SIERRA CLUB EXHIBIT FORMAT SERIES

Winner of the Carey-Thomas Award in 1964
for the best achievement in creative publishing in the United States

EDITED BY DAVID BROWER

THE WILD CASCADES

DAVID SIMONS: *Storm, Agnes country*

PHILIP HYDE: *Toward Canyon Lake from Miners Ridge*

The Harsh Country

There was a hardness of stone,
And uncertain glory,
Glitter of basalt and mica,
And the sheen of ravens.

. . .

Between cliffs of light
We strayed like children,
Not feeling the coarse shale
that cut like razors,

...

BOB and IRA SPRING: White Rock Lake

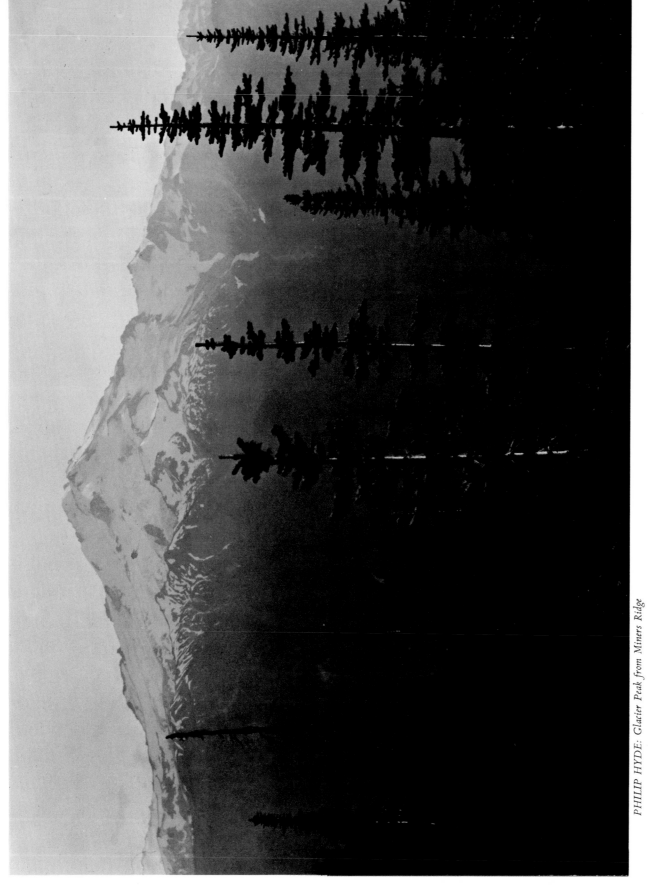

PHILIP HYDE: *Glacier Peak from Miners Ridge*

For a blond hill beckoned
Like an enormous beacon,
Shifting in sea change,
Not even farther.

Yet for this we travelled
With hope, and not alone,
In the country of ourselves.

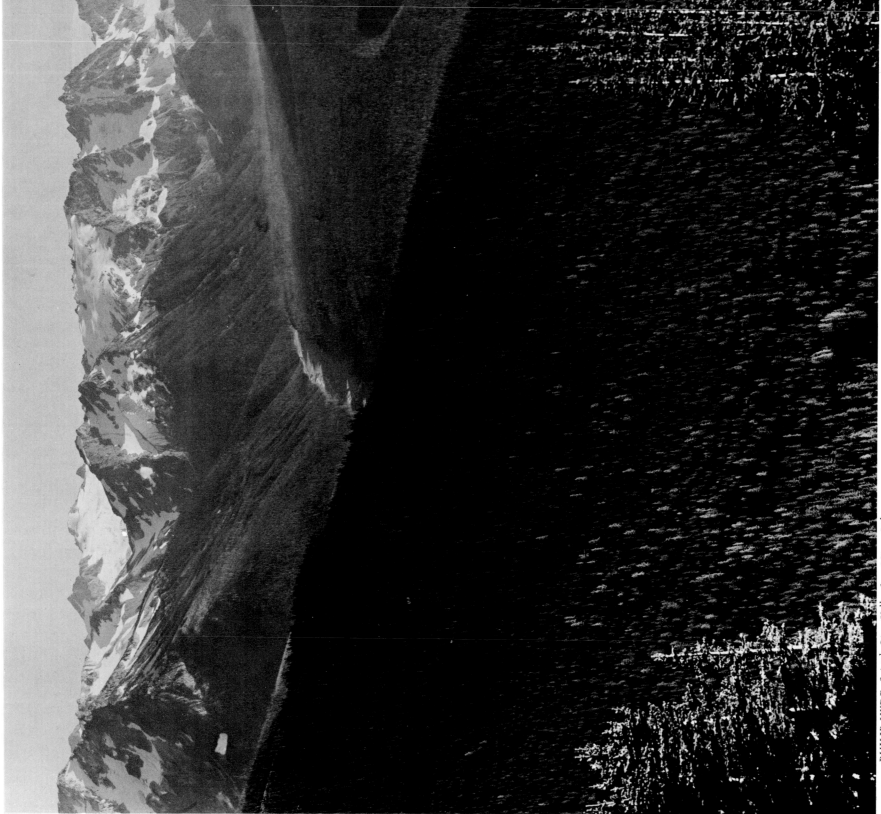

PHILIP HYDE: *Suiattle River Valley from Miners Ridge*

I long for the imperishable quiet at the heart of form.

The
Wild Cascades
FORGOTTEN PARKLAND

by HARVEY MANNING

photographs by ANSEL ADAMS, PHILIP HYDE,
DAVID SIMONS, BOB and IRA SPRING,
CLYDE THOMAS, JOHN WARTH, and others

with lines from THEODORE ROETHKE

foreword by WILLIAM O. DOUGLAS

edited by DAVID BROWER

ELEVENTH IN THE EXHIBIT-FORMAT SERIES

SIERRA CLUB · SAN FRANCISCO

Selections from Theodore Roethke

Publisher's Note: The book is set in Centaur and Arrighi. The color section and map are lithographed by Barnes Press Inc., New York, New York, and the black-and-whites in Futuratone by Kingsport Press Inc., Kingsport, Tennessee. The paper is Warren's Offset Enamel Gloss, bound in Columbia Mills' Sampson linen by Kingsport Press. The design is by David Brower.

The Sierra Club, founded in 1892 by John Muir, has devoted itself to the study and protection of national scenic resources, particularly those of mountain regions. All Sierra Club publications are part of the nonprofit effort the club carries on as a public trust. The club is affiliated with the International Union of Conservation, the Natural Resources Council of America, and the Federation of Western Outdoor Clubs. There are chapters in California, the Pacific Northwest, the Great Basin, the Rocky Mountains, the Southwest, the Great Lakes region, and on the Atlantic seaboard. Participation is invited in the program to enjoy and preserve wilderness, wildlife, forests, and streams. *Address: Mills Tower, San Francisco; 25 West 45 Street, New York; 712 Dupont Circle Building, Washington, D.C.*

PUBLICATIONS COMMITTEE, 1964-1965

AUGUST FRUGÉ, *Chairman;* GEORGE MARSHALL, *Vice Chairman;* ANSEL ADAMS, CHARLES B. HUESTIS, MARTIN LITTON, ROBERT L. USINGER, WILLIAM E. SIRI (*ex officio, President of the club*); DAVID BROWER, *Executive Director;* HUGH NASH, *Secretary;* CLIFFORD J. RUDDEN

Copyright, 1965 by the Sierra Club   Library of Congress Catalog Card No. 65-25632
Manufactured in the United States of America

All selections from the work of Theodore Roethke are fragments unless the title of the poem is shown. [The following poems, however, are continued, in sequence, in successive spreads: "The Harsh Country," "The Cycle," and "The Right Thing."]

The poems, or excerpts from them, entitled, "The Cycle," copyright 1941 by *The Virginia Quarterly Review, The University of Virginia:* "Carnations," "Moss-Gathering," copyright 1946 by Editorial Publications, Inc.: "Dolor," copyright 1943 and 1946 by Modern Poetry Association, Inc.: "A Field of Light," copyright 1948 by *The Tiger's Eye;* "A Light Breather," "The Visitant," "The Shape of the Fire," "Cuttings (later)," "I Cry, Love! Love!," "Words for the Wind," "A Walk in Late Summer," "What Can I Tell My Bones?", and "The Pure Fury," copyright 1947, 1948, 1950, 1955, 1957, 1958 by Theodore Roethke. All from the book, *Words for the Wind* by Theodore Roethke. All reprinted by permission of Doubleday & Company, Inc.

"The Sequel," "The Far Field," "The Abyss," "A Field of Light," "The Manifestation" ("Many Arrivals"), "The Rose," "The Longing," "The Long Waters," "Once More, The Round," "The Pike," and "The Right Thing," copyright 1960, 1962, 1963 by Beatrice Roethke as administratrix of the estate of Theodore Roethke. All from the book, *The Far Field* by Theodore Roethke. All reprinted by permission of Doubleday & Company, Inc.

"The Harsh Country" copyright 1959 by *The New Yorker.*

Excerpts from the prose are all from *The Poet and His Craft: Selected Prose of Theodore Roethke,* and fragments on pages 38, 40, and 69 herein are copyright 1965 by Beatrice Roethke as administratrix of the estate of Theodore Roethke, the former reprinted by permission of the University of Washington Press.

Acknowledgment

DAVID SIMONS spent two full summers in the Cascades and from his experience, notes, maps, photographs, and genius produced a brief and set a course that led to the conservationist consensus for establishing a national park there. He probed the region for yet another summer, spending so much of his time in behalf of Cascade conservation that his grades fell and his military deferment lapsed. In the army, late in 1960, he died of a sudden illness.

It is still hard to understand how a man so young could perceive and achieve so much so soon as he did in his Cascades work, both in Oregon and Washington. His drive and good-humored persistence moved mountains of apathy. His grasp and scope were of a rare kind. His collection of notes, negatives, prints, and unfinished manuscript, in the club's archives through the generosity of his parents, will be of recurring help in the years to come. If a North Cascades National Park is established, as it ought to be, it could not have happened if he had not contributed what he did.

Among his many achievements, Grant McConnell stimulated David Simons and started the club on its Cascades outings and book. His article in the 1956 *Sierra Club Bulletin*, "The Cascades Wilderness," introduced the club's members to "a sanctuary," as he put it, "one of the country's last and perhaps its greatest." He was forced to conclude that the Forest Service's "multiple-use policy can be made relevant to the needs of today only if it is re-founded on a determination to preserve the values that are essential to a healthy civilization and on a recognition that all values cannot be mixed without the extinction of some by others. Many areas can properly support a mingling of logging, grazing, recreation, and other uses. A few areas, those in which wilderness and scenic grandeur are of a superlative order, must be zoned for their highest purpose and exploitation firmly excluded." He felt that "These are not the playgrounds of the nation," but something transcendingly more. He believed that what happened in such places was an issue "nowhere of greater importance than in the Cascades Wilderness. A region as splendid as any in the nation, one unique in alpine character and beauty, has by accident been preserved as real wilderness." Could intelligence now carry on where accident had played out?

In the *Bulletin* two years later, Harold Bradley, then the club's president, amplified the basic issue:

"The Forest Service points out that our great timber resources for the future lie in the South and in the nation's idle or half-used woodlots [and in millions of acres of nonreforested non-tree farms, he might have added]. If that is so, should anyone rush to lumber the Cascade valleys? Why not keep their forests for their great aesthetic value as a beautiful foreground for the magnificent mountain picture, as a superlative, everlasting recreational resource? Timber will still be there if a national emergency should ever require it, and so with minerals, forage, dams, and highway routes....

"Respect for preservation comes to a culture somewhat as it comes to a man. In his infancy, beauty or other intangible values do not register—he will smear an old newspaper or a rare painting with equal gusto. Some years later he at least respects his parents' evaluation of the painting and lets it survive. In maturity he will delight in a painting, know that it is worth far more than a yard of canvas, a pound of paint, and wages. Perhaps it would be the last thing he would sacrifice.

"... I think we have matured enough to seek commodities elsewhere and let the Northern Cascades masterpiece survive unspoiled for those who we should assume will surely mature enough to cherish it. We can save for them, in this wilderness, our greatest national park."

The intervening years' battle for a park has put us in debt deeply:

To Harvey Manning, who in March agreed to try to produce a manuscript for *The Wild Cascades* for June publication. A Cascades explorer, writer, and editor, he had the capability but many conflicting commitments too. However, the Cascade River flows through the arteries on his right side and the Stehekin on his left, as any careful reader will readily perceive. So he made his deadline. The manuscript delighted all who reviewed it. Its form channeled the flow of photographs, and this in turn eddied with the poetry. The symbiosis is new to the series and makes the most of the sparkle that Harvey Manning has within him, in addition to those two rivers.

To Justice William O. Douglas for finding time between decisions and far-off places to write a foreword about a region he loves; to Patrick Goldsworthy and J. Michael McCloskey for many roles; to Noel McGary for an extraordinary map; to the photographers whose work we have used.

To the other photographers whose work we should have used; to the other authors and editors who helped us attain what we have here, even though they didn't write it—Grant McConnell and Weldon F. Heald, both of whom contributed enormously of their time, and to Charles B. Hessey, Jr., Ray Courtney, Edith Hardin English, Paul Tschirley, Joseph Hall, and Dee Molenaar, who wrote for us too.

To a host of conservationists in sister organizations, with

special reference to Dr. Goldsworthy and Philip H. Zalesky in the North Cascades Conservation Council; Polly Dyer, Chester Powell, Paul Wiseman, Leo Gallagher, and William R. Halliday in The Mountaineers; Alfred Schmitz, Bill and Margaret Oberreuffer, and Donald McKinley of the Mazamas; and Karl and Ruth Onthank of the Obsidians; to the clusters of friends in the other groups that constitute the Federation of Western Outdoor Clubs.

To Fred M. Packard, Bruce M. Kilgore, Sigurd Olson, C. Edward Graves, and Anthony Wayne Smith of the National Parks Association; to the Wilderness Society's Howard Zahniser, Irving Clark, and Robert Marshall, who helped while they lived, and to Harvey Broome, George Marshall, Charles G. Woodbury, John B. Oakes, and Stewart Brandborg, who help now; to friends in the other organizations who cooperated within the Natural Resources Council of America—especially Carl Buchheister and Charles Callison of the National Audubon Society, Joseph Penfold of the Izaak Walton League of America; Ira Gabrielson and Clinton Raymond Gutermuth and Dan Poole of the Wildlife Management Institute and Thomas L. Kimball and Louis S. Clapper of the National Wildlife Federation; Horace M. Albright of the American Planning and Civic Association; to the special friends of small wild places in the Nature Conservancy, and of big high places in the American Alpine Club and the Appalachian Mountain Club.

To the agency people who helped us get the facts—in the Forest Service, in the National Park Service, and more recently in the Bureau of Outdoor Recreation, as well as to the friends of the Cascades in the Secretary of the Interior's National Parks Advisory Board and in the study teams under the Outdoor Recreation Resources Review Commission, of which the club is a parent.

To the members of the Washington delegation in Congress who gave us encouragement, but especially Senators Henry M. Jackson and Warren Magnuson and Congressman Tom Pelly and their staffs.

To those who gave financial help, with special thanks to Thomas H. Wiancko, Dorothy and the late Russell Varian, and to Abigail Avery, together with the many contributors to our Cascades Fund and our Conservation and Memorial Fund, drawn upon to assist this book; to the bookbuyers who years ago started ordering it, cash in advance, on faith.

To those unnamed, whose support, unlike my memory, did not falter.

Our serendipity, and yours perhaps, comes from the keenness of a major American poet, the late Theodore Roethke. John Schanhaar first thought of putting our photographs to Roethke music. The poet's widow, Beatrice Roethke, brought to bear her knowledge of his work and of his Northwest; her suggestions have greatly improved the counterpoint. We have drawn principally from *Words for the Wind* and *The Far Field*, but also from *On the Poet and His Craft; Selected Prose of Theodore Roethke*, edited by Ralph J. Mills, Jr. (University of Washington Press). The editor's introductory remarks say of Roethke: "…he was, as even the lightest perusal of his poems will amply demonstrate, a writer who, in the practical sphere, carried out—and how beautifully and successfully too!—some of the most astonishing

experiments in the history of modern verse. At the same time, he maintained, as the other side of his poetic endeavor, a commitment to the traditional lyric…."

In Roethke's "Some Self-Analysis," written while he was a student at Michigan, we see why his lines blend as well as they do here:

"I have a genuine love of nature. It is not the least bit affected, but an integral and powerful part of my life. I know that Cooper is a fraud—that he doesn't give a true sense of the sublimity of American scenery. I know that Muir and Thoreau and Burroughs speak the truth.

"I can sense the moods of nature almost instinctively. Ever since I could walk, I have spent as much time as I could in the open. A perception of nature—no matter how delicate, how subtle, how evanescent,—remains with me forever. . . .

"I do not have the divine urge to write. There seems to be something surging within,—a profound undercurrent of emotion. Yet there is none of that fertility of creation which distinguishes the real writer.

"Nevertheless, I have faith in myself. I'm either going to be a good writer or a poor fool."

Many years later, in "On 'Identity,'" Roethke's feeling about the kind of things that keeps the Sierra Club busy comes through:

"I think we Americans . . . continue to make a fetish of 'thing-hood,' we surround ourselves with junk, ugly objects endlessly repeated in an economy dedicated to waste. Hence the possible relevance of my quotation from 'Dolor,' which I repeat in part:

I have known the inexorable sadness of pencils,
Neat in their boxes, dolor of pad and paper-weight, . . .
And I have seen dust from the walls of institutions,
Finer than flour, alive, more dangerous than silica,
Sift, almost invisible, through long afternoons of tedium,
Dropping a fine film on nails and delicate eyebrows,
Glazing the pale hair, the duplicate gray standard faces.

" '. . . We think by feeling. What is there to know?' This, in its essence, is a description of the metaphysical poet who thinks with his body: an idea for him can be as real as the smell of a flower or a blow on the head. And those so lucky as to bring their whole sensory equipment to bear on the process of thought grow faster, jump more frequently from one plateau to another more often."

In conflict as we must often be with what Galbraith calls the Conventional Wisdom, we are grateful for what Roethke's genius contributes, for the added dimension he gives our book. It will be gratifying if it helps people understand and work in, or work with, what the club works for: *We shall seek a renewed stirring of love for the earth; we shall urge that what man is capable of doing to the earth is not always what he ought to do; and we shall plead that all Americans, here, now, determine that a wide, spacious, untrammeled freedom shall remain in the midst of the American earth as living testimony that this generation, our own, had love for the next.*

Executive Director

San Francisco, June 28, 1965

CLYDE THOMAS: *Across the Agnes, from near Cloudy Pass*

It is no trick of change or chance of light.
A tree all out of shape from wind and rain,
A tree thinned by the wind obscures my sight.
The long day dies; I walk the woods alone,
Beyond the ridge two wood thrush sing as one.
Being delights in being, and in time,
The evening wraps me, steady as a flame.

[13]

Foreword

SEVERAL YEARS AGO, while sitting atop Plummer Mountain and looking to the whiteness of Glacier Peak and to the greenness of the Suiattle forests, I wondered whether the next generation would ever have the chance to experience the same feeling of serenity and composure that was mine at that moment. Would enough people learn of the beauties of this mountain wilderness, and soon enough, to preserve it from civilization pressing in from all sides? Or would the miners and loggers and others turn all this glory to the utilitarian appetites of man, leaving mere remnants to satisfy no less important human needs?

The questions remain unanswered; and in this book they are restated with the pressing urgency that the situation demands. While not minimizing the continuing danger, I am, however, much more optimistic now than I was at the time of my Plummer ascent. The North Cascades, then almost unknown beyond the immediate environs, have since become familiar to thousands of hillwalkers throughout the nation. *Almost* enough people—and I stress the *almost*—have now joined their efforts in a concerted campaign to establish a North Cascades National Park. But the time is not yet. The purpose of this book is to assemble the reinforcements needed to complete the campaign successfully.

As a people, our present attitude toward wilderness is ambivalent. Our nation was born in wilderness and was shaped in character by the interaction of civilization and wilderness. And for all time the great American epic is that of the frontier. It would be hard to find an adult American who does not feel nostalgia for the good old days, yet these are of two kinds. On the one hand are those who value wilderness for its own sake, as a place where a man can learn about his world and his place in it. On the other

hand are the few who value wilderness as a place where nature can be converted into riches, preferably without the hindrance of regulatory laws. Here, then, is the basic confrontation—between those who wish to preserve the remaining islands of American wilderness so that the frontier experience will continue to be available to future generations, and those few who want to exploit the wild lands in the uncontrolled manner of their grandfathers.

Our time, in America, is pivotal in regard to wilderness. Pockets of wilderness remain—bypassed and surrounded by the waves of civilization. But those islands are now in the mopping up stage. Roads are moving inward on these surrounding pockets, up a valley here, over a mountain there, along rivers. Yet though these pockets of wilderness are small by comparison with the frontier days when most of the continent was wild, until very recently —and strongly in the memory of many of us—they seemed very large and indestructible by virtue of their size and because they were rugged and forbidding.

Two alarming things are happening. First, the pockets of wilderness have been eroded at an increasing rate, with the help of our new technology. Second, as the population rises and the crowding intensifies, the need for wilderness grows. And looking forward into the years of the yet-uncontained population explosion, we can see that before control devices become operative (as they must become, or the whole question of wilderness becomes moot, and all our heirs will live in tall apartment houses and Central Park will be the wilderness prototype) the population will reach a point where far more wilderness is needed than is now planned to be saved.

Today we look backward to a time when there was more wilderness than the people of America needed. Today we look forward (and only a matter of a few years) to a time when *all* the wilderness now existing will not be enough.

It would, I think, be wise right now to stop all new roadbuilding into wild lands, all damming of wild rivers, all logging of virgin forests. The Americans of 2000 A.D. will thank us if we take that course.

If we do not preserve the remaining samples of primitive America, we will sacrifice traditional American values, the values of frontier America. Not every citizen goes to the wilderness—and they did not even 300 years ago. But so long as there is the presence of wilderness and the option of going to see it, a certain number of citizens do go there and bring back a message for their fellows. As long as that continues we will retain a historic connection with the past of our nation—and our race.

To repeat, what wilderness we decide to save within the next critical decade or two of decision-making will be all we will ever have. Probably it will not be enough. Probably it will be necessary, during the next century, to institute a program of reconstructing wilderness—that is to say, of setting areas aside and leaving them absolutely alone, after first removing such evidences of human "culture" as can be removed. We can evacuate the sheep and people and let the grass grow. But only nature can rebuild the ecological community proper to that individual area,

and this takes many, many years—in some places, centuries. It will not happen at all if man has removed and destroyed building blocks without which there can be no complete restoration. For all our science and technology, there is undoubtedly far more that we do not know about the critical elements of an ecosystem than we have yet learned.

The Northern Cascades happen to include a number of pockets of wilderness that for one reason or another have been bypassed, but are now under threat. Some say there is too much wilderness in the state of Washington. Parochial people say that Washington has so much that saving a certain percentage is enough. The wilderness of the North Cascades is a national resource of the future, not merely a local commodity, and we need it all, as a nation.

We need a number of protected wildernesses along the Cascade range—the Cougar Lakes Wilderness to help take care of the overflow from the Rainier Park, the Alpine Lakes Wilderness, the North Cascades Wilderness.

But we also need—and most of all—a North Cascades National Park. And that's the special message of this book.

WILLIAM O. DOUGLAS

Goose Prairie, Washington
June 20, 1965

I have come to a still, but not a deep center,
A point outside the glittering current;
My eyes stare at the bottom of a river,
At the irregular stones, iridescent sandgrains,
My mind moves in more than one place,
In a country half-land, half-water.

PHILIP HYDE: *Stream near Lyman Lake*

EDWIN J. DOLAN: *Head of Flat Creek*

So the abyss—
The slippery cold heights,
After the blinding misery,
The climbing, the endless turning,
Strike like a fire,
A terrible violence of creation,
A flash into the burning heart of the abominable;

Yet if we wait, unafraid, beyond the fearful instant,
The burning lake turns into a forest pool,
The fire subsides into rings of water,
A sunlit silence.

HOW MUCH I actually remember of my introduction to the North Cascades, and how much I remember remembering, or remember being told, is hard to say. We were camped beside the North Fork of the Stillaguamish, my father and mother and I. It was the middle of winter, freezing every night and all day in the shadows, but warm in the bright sun along the river. My parents fished most of the time, and I scrambled around digging holes in the sand and tossing rocks in the water and studying the construction of periwinkle shells. Sometimes I rode my father's shoulders right out into the middle of the river, and while he cast for steelhead I enjoyed the view of Whitehorse, the highest mountain in the world. All week long I examined the mountain carefully, not sure whether I was looking for a horse-like pattern of snowfields or a literal white horse prancing along the crest. Whichever it was, I never saw the horse. But I'm still looking.

My children can't possibly remember their first introductions to the North Cascades, since their camping began on family outings when the essential equipment included diapers and bottles and teething biscuits. One of the earliest commands-requests learned by Eldest Daughter, just after those related to urgent physical needs, was "Go mountains!"—a cry she unfailingly raised when the sun was shining and she sensed from the way I was dressed that I was not going into the city. Among Middle Daughter's early memories, and one she still really and truly remembers, is a terrible hot day on the way home from Lake Anne, below Shuksan. She was thirsty and sweating and the trail had been tough enough to walk when it was flat but now it started steeply uphill to Austin Pass and just then she was stung by a yellowjacket and that was too much—throwing herself down in the heather, she wailed her firm and final decision to stay right there forever and never take another step. As for Number Three, she was only two years old at the time so it's unlikely she can remember hiking to Pelton Lake, and how she became so exhausted on the return that I carried her most of the last mile, and how once back at Basin Creek Camp she instantaneously revived, and fooled around beside the Stehekin River for another four hours, covering approximately as many miles after sunset as she had all day.

For a third of a century, dating from that winter week under Whitehorse, the North Cascades have been a Manning family affair and therefore I can't claim any altruistic motives in adding my voice to those who call for a new national park. It's personal business for me. It is for Eldest Daughter, Middle Daughter, and Number Three, also; in my readings of the literature I've never heard more passionate screams of outrage than theirs when we meet a logging truck in the forests of the Suiattle or one of our other favorite valleys.

If my generation, or that of my parents, had begun with their fervor at their age, we'd have long since had a North Cascades National Park. However, until the last fifteen or so years a logging truck was something of a rarity in most of the better valleys, and only a few hillwalkers saw any danger. When I joined The Mountaineers in 1948, and under the stimulus and leadership of the Climbing Course began to travel deep and high into the North Cascades, the general attitude of myself and most of my new-found climbing friends was that the wilderness was inexhaustible, and if one valley was logged, or two or three or a dozen, we could always escape to what seemed uncountable virgin valleys remaining. In my immediate circle of mountain companions "conservationists" were so notably rare as to be objects of curiosity, and I used to consider their sermons on the mount as eccentricities to be tolerated and enjoyed, as one enjoys a friend's odd devotion to yodeling or smoked oysters. What they said was doubtless true enough, but how on earth could anything be done about it?

Yet the growing obligato of bulldozers, chain saws, and logging trucks forced many of us to begin to listen soberly and carefully to the sermons, and ultimately to become disciples. Hiking up the White Chuck in 1948, on the way to a climb of Glacier Peak, I remember Dick Brooks complaining bitterly about the logging in progress. And he still is, because the logging continues, but the difference is that now not just Dick and a few others are complaining, but many thousands, myself included and also my children. Sitting amid the moraines of Boston Basin in 1950, at a basecamp for a climb of Forbidden, I remember John and Polly Dyer, newly arrived in the Northwest, telling horror stories about the Sierra Nevada, and saying it could happen—here, but also saying that something had been and was being done about it in the Sierra, and something could be done here, by us.

This is not the place to name all the prophets, major and minor, of North Cascades preservation, but for personal reasons I must name these three, though certainly their recruitment of the Mannings as conservationists is the very least of their works. I also want to express gratitude to Patrick D. Goldsworthy, President of the North Cascades Conservation Council, for his untiring and immeasurably important efforts on behalf of the wilderness and of parklands in general, and for his efforts on behalf of this particular book. Parts 10 and 11 are largely drawn from the portions of the *Prospectus for a North Cascades National Park* (North Cascades Conservation Council, Seattle, 1963) prepared by Pat and by J. Michael McCloskey, who until recently was Northwest Conservation Representative of the Federation of Western Outdoor Clubs. At other places, in other ways, I've borrowed from, and been inspired by, the two other principal authors of the *Prospectus*, Chuck Hessey and John Warth. Pat and his wife Jane also offered helpful comments on this manuscript-in-progress, as did Martin Litton and Dave Brower. George Marshall is the philosopher of wilderness who steadily called me back from byways of passion, and the historian of wilderness who insisted on a maximum of fact and a minimum of speculation, and the walker of wilderness who stimulated my imagination with his own insights and memories. Dwight Crowder and Rowland Tabor took time out from reading the galleys on their new book, *Routes and Rocks: Hikers' Guide to the North Cascades from Glacier Peak to Lake Chelan* (The Mountaineers, Seattle, 1965), to correct certain of the most flagrant geological and geographical errors. Whatever is poor and wrong here is my fault; they all did their best on short notice to make the copy good, true, and reasonably beautiful. Finally I would like to thank my wife, Betty, for savagely criticizing the various drafts and for preparing the bibliography (massively assisted by Pat Goldsworthy), and Penny, Becky, Claudia, and their young brother Harry for accepting a deferred beginning of our 1965 North Cascades season so that these words might be written.

H. M.

Cougar Mountain
May 1965

Contents

WITH NINETY ILLUSTRATIONS, NINETEEN IN COLOR   AND A FOUR-COLOR FOLDED MAP

Such quiet under the small leaves!—
Near the stem, whiter at root,
A luminous stillness.

Low Valley

Part 1

THE FIRST DAY must begin in a valley bottom—a low valley, as low as possible, no more than 1,000 feet above sealevel and preferably less than 2,500 feet above sealevel, and the only long view straight up to the sky between and beyond tall trees. A few steps from the summer brightness and dust of road's end, multi-layered branches lace together overhead, shadowing and cooling the trail, a two-foot-wide lane of civilization entering a wilderness many miles across and two miles high, and as wild now as when civilization began.

The morning trail passes Douglas firs too immense to walk by without pausing to see closely and sense deeply the tallness and the oldness, and hemlocks not much smaller or younger, and an occasional ancient cedar with massive root buttresses, fire-blackened trunk, and broken top—a monument of life-in-death shaped by centuries of slow growth and sudden violence. For every tree standing another dozen lie on the ground, some fresh-splintered, felled by the winds and snows of the past winter, others long since merged into soil and now become ridges of young hemlocks. The trail climbs far above the river on a dry sidehill, through salal and Oregon grape and the reek of sun-baked pine, drops into a dank gorge green with fronds of sword fern, deer fern, and maidenhair fern, and trenches through river-bank thickets of salmonberries in a grove of cottonwood and maple and alder footed in black leaf mould, branches and trunks swollen with moss.

A bend in the valley gives a glimpse out of the forest, up through haze to the ending of forest green and the beginning of meadow green streaked and patched with snow, a bright upper world impossibly remote from the low world of rivers, trees, and shadows. For morale's sake it is best to put away thoughts of so improbable a world, an infinity of footsteps away, and bury one's face in a creek and drink cold water in slow, lingering swallows, then lie back in moss, letting the sweat cool, and watch a thousand busy things with wings circle in a sunbeam.

The miles grow long in the afternoon, and the steps short and slow, and the rest stops frequent. The trail gains elevation, yet the forest is as full and tall as in the morning; the trail crosses tributaries, yet the river is no less loud. Forest and river are surely without end, and in all the knowable wilderness the maximum goal is a riverside bench with humus for a mattress and a gravel bar for a kitchen, and a log for a seat and a fire for warmth and light in a cold night that fills the valley even before the sky is dark enough for stars.

Thus ends the first day, as deep in forest as it began, and not much higher above sealevel. This is the *valley* day, the mandatory beginning for a respectful entry into the North Cascades.

Next morning the trail abruptly switchbacks up a step in the valley, the river composed of equal parts of air and water, a series of pounding cascades and bubbling plunge basins, white foam and green pools. At the top of the step the trail emerges for the first time into full sunshine, crossing a green flood of slide alder and willow and vine maple sweeping down from gray talus thousands of feet above. Once again in forest, the silver fir are still thick at the base but dwindling in height, and with short, steep branches; the shadows are not deep enough to be cool and the hot air is heavy with resin, and it is important now to inspect the huckleberry bushes, watching for ripe blue fruit.

Again the trail opens out into the sun, this time onto a causeway of cedar puncheon crossing a meadow-marsh where slow streams meander through fields of knee-high grass, and frogs leap from underfoot and splash in stagnant ponds squirming with polliwogs, and the air is rank with the smell of skunk cabbage and black ooze.

Late in the afternoon the trail climbs another valley

step, and once more, and this time finally, emerges from the forest, emerges from premature dusk into the brilliance of heather and flowers and rock and snow and a suddenly enormous sky. The alpine firs no longer are continuous but climb the valley walls as narrow strips between avalanche paths and cluster in small groups atop knolls. And when the trail comes to the river, it is not the thunderer of the lower valley; in fact, it's not a river at all, but only one fragment of the river which here is gathering itself together from waterfalls streaming down cliffs from hanging valleys and perched snowfields.

With campfire beside a torrent boiling out from under the snow, with tarp strung from alpine firs, with flowers and grass and heather extending all around to moraines and snows and ice-plucked buttresses, with marmots whistling in the alpenglow, here in the upper world that as recently as morning seemed impossible of attainment, here ends the second day, the transition day essential to a respectful North Cascades entry.

Having paid one's way with many thousand steps and many pints of sweat, having learned to know the forest and river well, the third day is the summit day, duly earned —a day of strolling through meadows and scree to a pass or a peak, looking out over mountains and glaciers—and down to valleys dimmed by the blue haze exhaled by the living forest. High in sunshine, high in the quiet air of the upper wilderness, it is difficult to conceive that at the feet of those trees is the green gloom and the river roar of yesterday and the day before, that the high world of wide horizons and minute flowers and the low world of deep shadows and giant trees and loud water are, indeed, parts of the same world, the unified world of wilderness mountains.

After such a properly respectful North Cascades entry, it is at length necessary to exit, and this too in a properly respectful manner. Again there is a transition day, taking leave of the last snowfield, the last heather, the last near view of rock and ice, watching the river grow on the way down, and watching the trees grow, and the shadows.

The final day is, as was the first, a forest day, and the Douglas fir and hemlock and cedar seem marvelously gigantic after the days spent above where plants are miniaturized for survival, where only the peaks and glaciers and sky are huge. There comes a final glimpse of snow-streaked green meadows far above in haze, once more receding into improbability. And then the trail ends, and while the traveler washes his feet in the loud river, all the louder after the quiet of high ridges, he may speculate whether some of the cold water rushing through his toes may not, mere hours ago, have melted from the snowfield at his meadow camp.

A path went walking.
The sun glittered on a small rapids.
Some morning thing came, beating its wings.
The great elm filled with birds.

Listen, love,
The fat lark sang in the field;
I touched the ground, the ground warmed by the killdeer,
The salt laughed and the stones;
The ferns had their ways, and the pulsing lizards,
And the new plants, still awkward in their soil,
The lovely diminutives.

I could watch! I could watch!
I saw the separateness of all things!
My heart lifted up with the great grasses;
The weeds believed me, and the nesting birds.
There were clouds making a rout of shapes crossing a windbreak of cedars,
And a bee shaking drops from a rain-soaked honeysuckle.
The worms were delighted as wrens.
And I walked, I walked through the light air;
I moved with the morning.

PHILIP HYDE: Fall on Park Creek

The Cycle

Dark water, underground,
Beneath the rock and clay,
Beneath the roots of trees,
Moved into common day,
Rose from a mossy mound
In mist that sun could seize.

. . .

PHILIP HYDE: *Upper White Chuck Basin*

The fine rain coiled in a cloud
Turned by revolving air
Far from that colder source
Where elements cohere
Dense in the central stone,
The air grew loose and loud.

. . . .

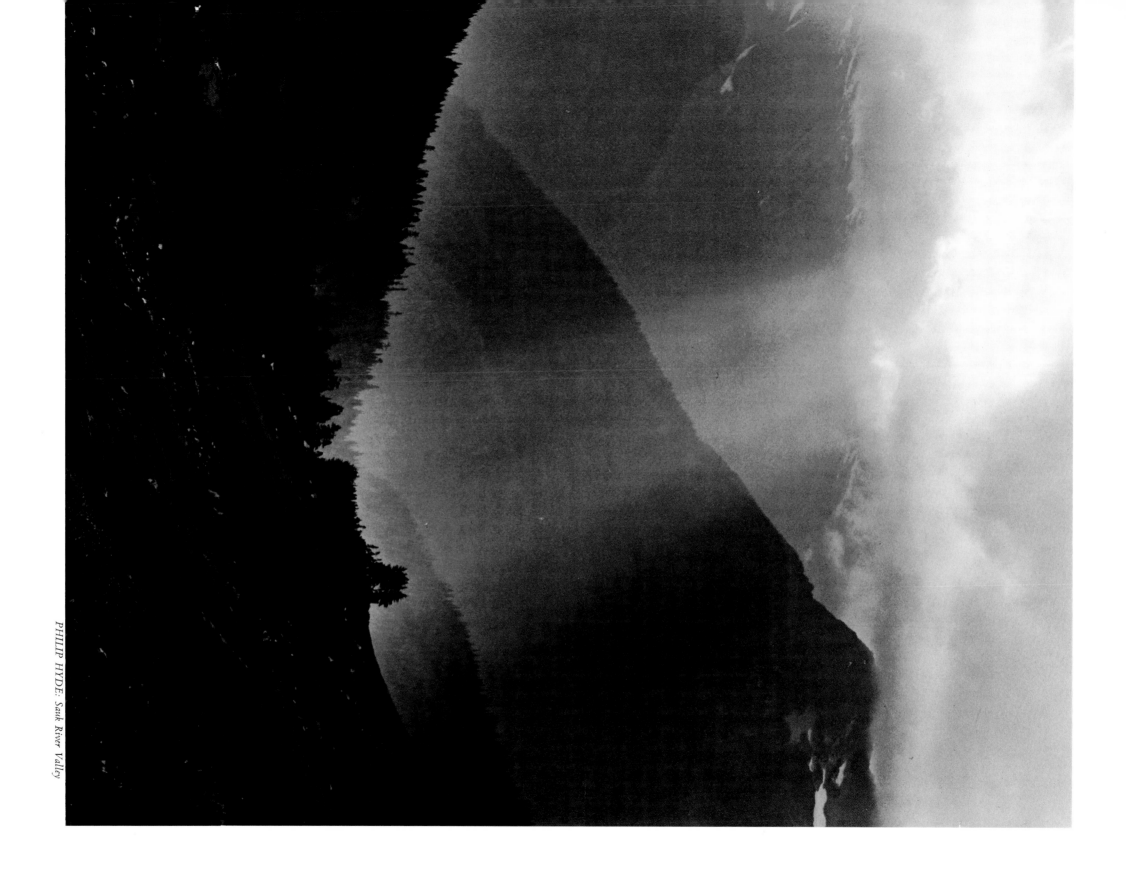

PHILIP HYDE: *Sauk River Valley*

ANSEL ADAMS: Stump and Mist, near Cascade Pass

Then, with diminished force,
The full rain fell straight down,
Tunnelled with lapsing sound
Under even the rock-shut ground
Under a river's source,
Under primeval stone.

Part 2

Rain Sleep

No SLEEP is so peaceful as wilderness sleep, rain sleep. City anxieties cannot follow beyond the sound-range of internal combustion machines, and are submerged too deep to clutter and muddle the calm flow of wilderness dreams. And while rain continues there is no pack to carry, altitude to gain, brush to fight, route to find. Possibly the only pure and quiet sleep remaining for civilized man is a rain sleep in the wilderness, an island in time.

Rain sleep is not deep sleep, not after twenty or thirty or forty more-or-less continuous hours in the sleeping bag, but rather a shallow half-sleep, a blend of fragrances and sounds of forest and river and memories of other wilderness days and nights. The sleeper hears the steady roar of the river and he dreams of this and a hundred other remembered rivers, and as he dreams the unified sound of the river separates into scores of distinct sounds from individual rapids and ripples, all flowing into a whole and complete dream of rivers present and past.

The sleeper also hears the rain on the tarp, which moment to moment and hour to hour varies from a steady rattle to a sporadic pit-a-pat, and he hears the hiss of wind through the branches as each new wave of rain arrives, and he smells the wetness of fir needles inches from his nose, and feels breezes on his cheek, and all this and much more enters the snug dreams of rain in the wilderness.

Sleep is a central pleasure of the North Cascades, and also an indispensable technique, for though the respectful three-day entry is ideal, it is even more respectful and much more realistic to plan a four-day entry (or five, or six) with the extra day or more spent in a valley forest, under a tarp, asleep. To argue with the weather, to consider the extra day or more wasted, is to be a maladjusted alien, irritable and miserable. To be a comfortable and happy citizen, a traveler must be able not only to sleep out the nights, which even the novice can do, but must learn how to sleep away the days, perhaps several in a row.

However, for insomniacs who do nothing but toss and turn after twenty or thirty hours in the bag, and for skillful sleepers seeking a change of pace, there are other useful ways to spend a rainy day in a wet forest. One can sit under an overhanging log and visually catalog the splashes and ripples and swirls which add together into the total roar of the river; or dissect its complex texture by tossing twigs in the water and tracing their routes through falls and eddies and backwaters. For variety, periodically a dipper will materialize on a spray-drenched boulder, bounce limberly at the knees a moment, then flit up or down the river avenue, inches from the water, and perhaps dive into a waterfall, and perhaps explode out again, and perhaps—mysteriously—not.

Or one can lie under the tarp and examine the forest tree by tree, and within its narrow range of subdued greens and blacks find color subtleties never caught by camera, nor even by the human eye except in such leisurely, drowsy exploration. And there is no better way to sink back into sleep than watching raindrops, the misty ones drifting down and down from low gray clouds, and the fat ones plunging heavily from branches.

Or one can recall that "rain is only water and the skin is waterproof" and go walking in the forest, and find that after completing the initial process of getting soaking wet, all the way to the skin, there is no more pain remaining in the rain, or the water-heavy brush, or even knee-deep streams, and one can then proceed pleasurably through the watery wilderness with a sort of swimming motion, winking the excess rain out of the eyes, blowing drips from the upper lip, and lulled by the rhythmic squish in the boots.

This extra day (or two, or three) has another value.

There is the chance that rain will continue and vacation time run out, and one will return to the city with a week's worth of forest memories, river memories, rain memories, and never a single minute of heather memories. The fact that this may happen on any trip, and that statistically it *will* on a certain proportion of trips, releases a particular fierce joy when the sun returns, if it does.

Moreover, when the eye and the mind have become accustomed to the muted reality of valley-rain greens and grays, they cannot cope—except through temporary hysteria—with the sun-charged super-reality of green grass, blue sky, white snow, brown moraine, and the myriad explosions of color spattered through the meadow. The bland sanity of forest rain is the necessary pre-condition of absolute alpine mania.

For balance, some days of rain should be spent in the high country rather than the low, and here particularly the proper North Cascades shelter is not a womb-like tent but a tarp with all-around picture windows and breeze-ways that allow intimate enjoyment, awake and asleep, of earth and sky. Furthermore, the tarp-camper has a more watchful intimacy with the weather, since once in every so many trips there will come a storm designed specifically for tents, a horizontal storm that blows rain under the tarp as well as above—or perhaps flaps it to shreds.

A meadow sleep in rain or fog has a special feeling of quiet isolation, yet never the deep serenity of a valley sleep, for always there is the threat of storm. Also there are mysteries, and questions, such as whether there is, any more, a world beyond the cloud, or only void; or whether in escaping the city one accidentally destroyed it, and is

now condemned to solipsism. So it is that even the most skilled sleeper becomes restless during a wet day in the high country.

One can walk out into fog and focus on the view underfoot, undistracted by crowded horizons, and examine rocks crystal by crystal rather than cliff by cliff, and trace the path of a spider climbing up and down the suncups in a snowfield, and the contortions of grain in a bleached log, the flight of droplets in a waterfall, the black lines of an alpine fir etched in white mist, and experience flowers one by one, petal by petal, rather than in a thousand-flowered medley of meadow color, and thus, in the words of William Blake, "see the world in a grain of sand, all heaven in a wild flower."

And when a hole opens in the clouds, however briefly, the glimpsed peak, glacier, or valley is a feast, and every detail of cliff, crevasse, or forest is devoured with the hunger of long anticipation, there being no competition from rich hundreds of peaks and glaciers and valleys.

Always, too, there are such camp pleasures as the warmth of fire on fog-chilled knees and the slow sipping of a cup of hot soup. However, the sure sign of an alien is that he spends days of alpine rain drying socks, or more often charring them. The true citizen of the North Cascades aims only to keep dry the small patch of heather under the tarp, and with it the sleeping bag and the food. So long as there is water in the sky there will be water in socks and boots, and not until the sun returns will pants and shirt and sweater and parka ever be entirely dry. However, having come originally from the sea, man with his waterproof skin can learn to live wet. In the North Cascades, he must.

Pale blossoms, each balanced on a single jointed stem,
The leaves curled back in elaborate Corinthian scrolls;
And the air cool, as if drifting down from wet hemlocks,
Or rising out of ferns not far from water,
A crisp hyacinthine coolness,
Like that clear autumnal weather of eternity,
The windless perpetual morning above a September cloud.

JOHN F. WARTH: False hellabore on Miners Ridge; Glacier Peak

JOHN F. WARTH: *Skagit Valley from Sauk Mountain*

. . . I hear a river's undersong,
In a place of mottled clouds, a thin mist morning and evening.
I rock between dark and dark,
My soul nearly my own,
My dead selves singing.
And I embrace this calm—

Part 3

Transition

IDEALLY the valley day, transition day, and summit day of a North Cascades entry should be linked end to end along a single trail. However, without ever hiking more than a few miles—or in the extreme case without hiking at all—one can experience the integrated whole of valley and peak, forest and meadow, river and snow; even on the fringes of a wilderness one can sense the inner immensity and from it gain personal strength, or new understanding of how the world operates, or what one will.

For an easy valley day there is the rain forest of Sulphur Creek, a leisurely hour's walk each way to the hot springs, or else a long, rich day if one moves from one enormous tree to the next, one lush bank of moss and ferns to the next, pausing to give each day due justice. There are also the Suiattle trail, and the North Fork Sauk trail, and the White River trail, and the Thunder Creek trail, and a score of others that lead into cool green-gloomy shadows. And at innumerable places along the Cascade, Chiwawa, Early Winters, and other rivers and creeks, no more than a few steps from the automobile one can find a soft seat of moss or needles with a Douglas fir or Ponderosa pine backrest and while away a serene afternoon of river-watching, dipper-watching.

For a summit day there is Cascade Pass, an afternoon's stroll from the road, with the heather-banked ponds and alpine hemlocks of Mixup Arm and the steep greenery of Sahale Arm, and the hanging glaciers on the mile-high wall of Johannesberg.

Or the Sibley Creek trail, switchbacking from forest into grass and flowers, and giving access—by means of a short meadow-scramble—to a saddle overlooking the trees of the Cascade River and all its tributaries, and the rock and ice of Little Devil, Baker, Big Devil, Shuksan, Eldorado, Logan, Buckner, Forbidden, Boston, Johannesberg, Formidable, Dome, Glacier, Buckindy, Snowking, and a score of other peaks with names, and several score more without.

And in the meadows of Austin Pass on the west or Harts Pass on the east, one can—from the automobile window, if need be—look out over portions of a mountain wilderness that extends from Stevens Pass on the south into Canada on the north, and from tidewater lowlands of Puget Sound on the west to inland semi-deserts of the Columbia Plateau on the east, an alpine wilderness far and away the largest in all the contiguous United States.

For transition days there are the approaches to these summit days, and also hundreds of other approaches, short and long, most by foot but some by automobile—but it cannot be stressed too emphatically that the only way to know the land is to move slowly through it, and when travel is by automobile there must be frequent lengthy stops along the way or the transition is too swift to be respectful and the experience is lost. To step out into meadows a few hasty hours from the city is like having a feast of ice cream and cookies without first enjoying the soup, salad, and steak.

Thus, even the traveler unable to walk any considerable distance can link valleys, transitions, and summits of the North Cascades into a complete entry, bottom to top; all that is required is respect. During a week or two spent driving around the perimeter of the rough square, approximately 100 miles on a side, that contains most of the wilderness, and probing valley roads from such gateway towns as Glacier, Marblemount, Darrington, Granite Falls, Cashmere, Entiat, Chelan, and Twisp, one can come to know the North Cascades in a way comparable to those who link their entry days together on the White Chuck, Entiat, Little Beaver, or other trails.

To be sure, total wilderness immersion comes only on deep-probing foot journeys days and nights distant from the road, but just as one need not rocket into space to learn something—learn much—from stars, one can stand on a wilderness border and from it learn however much lies within one's innate spiritual capacity to learn. "Natural piety," as it has been called, is more significant than physical endurance: some gain North Cascades citizenship during a single day by the side of the road; others are born in or near the wilderness and spend long and active lives plundering it and remain always aliens, never knowing their homes, never caring.

The classic approach to the range—and unique for these and all other American mountains—is Lake Chelan, a body of water fifty miles long and at no point much beyond a mile from side to side, a lake that is more like a wide river, or a fjord. As the prelude to a march into the back country, or simply for the boat ride, Lake Chelan is fundamental to a full understanding of the North Cascades.

Both in history and myth man has considered the act of crossing water—ocean or river, Atlantic, Rubicon, or Styx—to have more than routine significance. In folklore there are demons and horrors forbidden by the terms of their existence to cross water, which therefore in some cases provides decent folk a sure escape from hot pursuit. Certainly some evil spirits—carbon monoxide and billboards and neon among them—have never yet survived the journey up Lake Chelan.

At the head of the lake is a town, Stehekin, and the outlet of a river, the Stehekin. A few score people live there the year around and they maintain a few miles of narrow, low-speed road along the valley and they keep several dozen automobiles and trucks of mixed vintage for their own use and for hire to summer visitors. But the town, and the "road which starts on a handsome lakeshore and dead-ends in Paradise," and the valley, are not dominated by the sounds of infernal combustion machines.

In the memory of men now living, and not so very old men at that, the water roads of the Northwest—the bays and inlets of Puget Sound and Admiralty Inlet and the Strait of Georgia, the rivers and lakes draining into the Columbia and Fraser—were the major or only travel routes to some parts of the country. For this reason the five-hour voyage in the *Lady of the Lake* from the town of Chelan to the town of Stehekin seems much longer—

longer by some fifty years journey into the past—because here is the only such water road to wilderness remaining, and the only wilderness-edge town where the water road is the only access—except by foot or by air—from the outside.

A North Cascades entry that begins with Lake Chelan has from the start an extra measure of history, even before the camping and walking begins. And the Stehekin is a valley where one can car-camp without a car—hiring a ride up the road, being dumped along the way to spend a week or two and then picked up at vacation's end. Between dump-out and pick-up, a party may walk along the forest trails of Agnes, Bridge, and Park Creeks, climb peaks from Glacier on the south to Goode and Logan on the north, fish the rivers and lakes, or possibly just sit by a river, looking, remembering the words of a Greek philosopher: "It is not possible to walk twice through the same river."

For one of the easiest available transition days there is the several-mile trail from the road-end forest at Cottonwood Camp up into meadows of Horseshoe Basin, where a dozen white lines of falling water inscribe the tall headwall of the lower cirque, and the glaciers and snowfields of the upper cirque are ringed by the 9,000-foot-or-near peaks of Sahale, Boston, Ripsaw Ridge, Buckner, and Booker—all first seen from the *Lady of the Lake*, down on the 1,100-foot surface of Lake Chelan.

And for a summit day there is again Cascade Pass, but a Cascade Pass unsuspected by travelers who know it only from approaches through the logging-scarred valleys of the west. By luck of geography and economics, the entire Stehekin River—from delta marshes in Lake Chelan to glaciers above Cascade Pass—has until now been preserved in very nearly its primitive condition. Here is still an opportunity to meet a virgin river at its ending and learn to know it through all its backward course to its numerous beginnings.

As a water-road entry into wilderness mountains, Lake Chelan is unique in America. As a complete wilderness entity of forest and meadow, free-flowing river and tributaries, water and ice, valley and peak, lake and glacier, the Stehekin is unique in America. In all the North Cascades, and in all America, the unit of Lake Chelan and the Stehekin River is one of a kind, and there can never be another.

A wind came close, like a shy animal.

JOHN F. WARTH: *Goodell Creek and Mount Despair*

Wilderness Thresholds

JOHN F. WARTH: Thunder Creek, Boston Glacier, and Mount Buckner

What I love is near at hand,
Always, in earth and air.

CLYDE THOMAS: *Lake Chelan and Domke Lake*

DAVID SIMONS: *Agnes Creek Valley from McGregor Mountain*

I walk in this great decay;
The woods wet by the wind,
The dying moss, the brown
Features of time's delay . . .

DAVID SIMONS: *Suiatle trail*

JOHN F. WARTH: *Diablo Lake and Colonial Peak*

The far slope of the range, half light, half shade,
The final man, his bones adrift in fire,
The dream extending beyond darkness and waste,
To see beyond the self
This quiet's but the means,
Whether it's found or lost.

PHILIP HYDE: *White River from White Pass*

Once More, the Round

What's greater, Pebble or Pond?
What can be known? The Unknown.
My true self runs toward a Hill
More! O More! visible.

Now I adore my life
With the Bird, the abiding Leaf,
With the Fish, the questing Snail,
And the Eye altering all;
And I dance with William Blake
For love, for Love's sake;

And everything comes to One,
As we dance on, dance on, dance on.

ANSEL ADAMS: *Stehekin River cedars*

[43

CLYDE THOMAS: "Trail" from Trapper Lake

Leaves, leaves, lean forth and tell me what I am . . .

Part 4

Cosmology

MANY A TRAVELER, through informed choice or by lucky chance, spends all his North Cascades vacations on well-kept trails that lead gently through forests to meadows to moraines to ice, and looks back upon the range in memory as a true museum of primitive America, but on the whole as serene and secure as any arboretum. Others, though, through boldness or ignorance, learn to appreciate fully why the term "*wild Cascades*" is used.

The lakes, waterfalls, and rivers, and the snowfields and glaciers, and the forests and flowers, and the clouds and fogs are what make the North Cascades a green and pleasant land, but sometimes one may reflect on the implications of 150 inches of annual precipitation, and realize that if it were all to come down at once, as rain, and not rush off immediately, a tall man standing on the shoulders of another tall man standing on a trail would still be drowning. Of course it does not all come down at once, and not all as rain, and not everywhere to a 150-inch total, and it spends all year rushing off—and thereby hangs many a tale. In less-frequented valleys, and even along heavily traveled routes early in summer, before the trail crew arrives, the "museum" is split into small segments by wild, wild rivers.

For many hikers (including virtually all wives) the major hazard of the range is footlogs. And surely only a determined candidate for martyrdom ventures blithely onto a log that has lost its bark and is greasy from spray, especially since styles in boot-soles changed, and tricouni nails went out of fashion and rubber lugs came in. Premeditation is essential when such a log spans a meltwater flood within whose loud roar one can hear the grinding and thumping of basketball-size boulders in motion, and dignity is abandoned in the act of embracing a log to begin a belly-squirm crossing. High-country footlogs are also challenging, for perhaps the water is not dangerously deep but quite plentiful enough to saturate the hiker and his pack, and perhaps the torrent is merely a dozen feet wide but the footlog is a limber alder three inches thick and all

one can do is start fast and keep moving, trusting inertia to overcome gravity.

When there is no footlog, nor reasonable hope of one, either the trip ends on the spot or the river must be forded, a pleasure when the day is hot and the stream of moderate depth and speed, but something else entirely when water boils to the hips or waist, pushing the half-floating body relentlessly downstream, when the feet slip on rounded boulders and the probing ice ax dislodges other boulders that smash the shins, and all the while the swift rush of close-to-the-eyes current tilts the horizon sideways. Moreover, those who lose footing and bounce a dozen yards down the river suffer an intensely lonely and personal trauma, because as seen from shore (by companions who have already crossed) the spectacle is entertaining, and the only way to get any sympathy is to drown.

The abundance of water nourishes the timeless prosperity of brush, and many two-foot lanes of civilization need be neglected by the trail crew only a summer or two to become intransigent wilderness again.

There are a number of varieties of brush, and each has its exponents as the most typical of the North Cascades. Some mention with respect a steep sidehill swamp in a forest canyon, with over-the-boots black ooze covering rock slabs, and down-slanting twigs and mushy mats of leaves supplied for additional skid surfaces, and crowning all a luxurious growth of poison-barbed devils club that must be grasped firmly to maintain balance. Some cite beaver ponds extending from river to cliff. Some remember blowdowns.

Others argue for an avalanche track liberally littered with a jackstraw of old and new logs and richly grown up in slide alder and vine maple. Travel is largely vertical, arm-hauling and leg-straddling onto head-high logs, then jumping down through greenery to unseen, ankle-twisting boulders. Forward progress, insofar as there is any, comes by pulling apart and squirming through knots of intertwined branches. In the densest portion of the avalanche should be a white-water torrent. And for completeness add a seasoning of nettles and a blistering of sun and a mist of mosquitoes and a fury of flies.

Whatever the variety, brush at its most typical must be not only of the highest quality, as brush goes, but in great quantity. There is value in crossing a single avalanche or devils club swamp, but the extreme test of faith is devoting an entire day to battling through a succession of avalanches, blowdowns, devils club swamps, and beaver ponds and at sunset being barely two miles from morning's camp. There are such valley jungles in the North Cascades —jungles that in all human history have been traveled only once or twice, and some perhaps not at all. Knowing this adds much to the enjoyment of certain high meadows. It is good to look down to (and not be in) a valley that is in every sense absolutely wild.

Streams in flood and brush, and also cliffs and glaciers and snowfields, guard many portions of the North Cascades from casual entry, and often enough storm fronts from the Pacific Ocean fence the entire range. But even along a first-class trail in clear, calm weather there is another element in the wildness of the North Cascades, and that is simply the vertical distance from the low forests to the high meadows. And in fact, the sunnier the weather the more formidable the barrier.

Some trails don't placidly follow valley bottoms, but abruptly leave the river and strike off directly for the high country. Generally, for good and proper (though inhumane) reasons of easy construction and maintenance, these trails follow south-facing slopes and scrupulously avoid watercourses. The Little Giant trail from the Chiwawa to the Napeequa, the Suiattle trail to Image Lake, and the North Fork Sauk trail to White Pass—the latter with an elevation gain of 3,000 feet, virtually every step of the way open to the sun, and with absolutely no late-summer water—are as spiritually purifying on bright days as any trial by brush.

For maximum effect the ascent should be made during settled weather an appropriate period of time following the passage of a packtrain. The heat rises in visible waves from the dust, evaporating perspiration faster than pores can produce it, drying the mouth to a hot sludge of glue and grit, and maddening the attending swarm of horse flies. There is no wind, and the trail rises too steeply for a hiker to stir the stagnant air by forward motion. There is no water, and the canteen supply must be reserved for emergency sips to keep the throat open. At length the knees buckle and the body of its own mindless volition topples to ground in the thin shade of a shriveled little tree. But there is no rest, for the flies close in and limp arms must flail constantly to prevent invasion of the eyes, nose, ears, and wide-open gasping mouth. On reaching White Pass from the Sauk, one understands why the meadows are not uniformly over-run with the crowds they merit.

Sometimes it is difficult to enter the North Cascades, and sometimes, too, it is difficult to exit. Not always is there opportunity for fond leavetaking of glaciers, moraines, heather, and flowers, pausing to savor memories of high country pleasure. One may go peacefully to sleep at White Rock Lakes, convinced after days of blue skies and gentle breezes that a world so kind can have no room for evil. But at midnight sleep is ended by a cannon-shot crack of the tarp, and the remainder of the night is a semi-conscious struggle to hold down the edges of the tarp and preserve the dryness of a few square feet of meadow. In a dim dawn comes yet another wave of wind, ninth of the ninth waves, that does not subside but grows, and when it can grow no more explodes and rips the tarp clean away, stripping the sleeping bags naked under the low, swift sky.

It is properly a day of hibernation, not walking, but wishful thinking has been abandoned and the storm accepted as a full-scale three-day blow. The escape route lies up over a cold, sodden glacier, and long before reaching the pass each traveler has ten pounds of sky-fresh water added to his clothing and pack. No gentle farewells now, not so much as a backward glance to White Rock Lakes and the Agnes, erased by gale-driven sleet, only an intense desire for the shelter of the Downey forest. But at this point the refugees lose the way and are trapped in a maze of ice-polished slabs with gray emptiness below—a trap escaped through blind fumbling that leads to steep meadows slashed by miniature canyons, each requiring a slithering descent suspended from handfuls of heather and a hand-over-hand clawing climb of the far wall. In the drenched grass and semi-fluid soil every foothold must be firmly kicked, but every third step fails, and the glissades down colorless flowers are arrested by toes and ice ax and loud groans of despair. When at last timberline is reached, and the blazes dropping to the valley bottom and the Downey Creek trail, one realizes why some North Cascades travelers prefer tents.

A week or two later, safely back in the city and all gear finally dry, one may look at photographs taken before the storm—views across the deep hole of the West Fork of Agnes Creek to Dome Peak and the Chickamin and Dana Glaciers—and be reminded of the cosmology of the *Divine Comedy*, and feel humbly certain that for those who have been to White Rock Lakes in sunshine and a three-day blow both the Paradise and Purgatory of Dante will be anticlimactic, and for those who have lost a tarp there not even his Inferno will seem wilder than the wild Cascades.

To stare into the after-light, the glitter left on the lake's surface,
When the sun has fallen behind a wooded island . . .

Living Space

PHILIP HYDE: *Glacier Peak from Image Lake*

DAVID SIMONS: Image Lake and Suiattle headwaters

To have the whole air!
The light, the full sun
Coming down on the flowerheads,
The tendrils turning slowly,
A slow snail-lifting, liquescent.

DAVID SIMONS: *Glacier Peak and Flower Dome from Buck Creek Pass*

PHILIP HYDE: Eldorado from Cascade Pass

All finite things reveal infinitude:
The mountain with its singular bright shade
Like the blue shine on freshly frozen snow,
The after-light upon ice-burdened pines;
Odor of basswood on a mountain-slope,
A scent beloved of bees;

    . . .

PHILIP HYDE: *Bonanza Peak and Lyman Lake*

Silence of water above a sunken tree:
The pure serene of memory in one man, —
A ripple widening from a single stone
Winding around the waters of the world.

JOHN F. WARTH: *Cooper Lake*

A single wave starts lightly and easily shoreward,
Wrinkling between reeds in shallower water,
Lifting a few twigs and floating leaves,
Then washing up over small stones.

The shine on the face of the lake
Tilts, backward and forward.
The water recedes slowly,
Gently rocking.

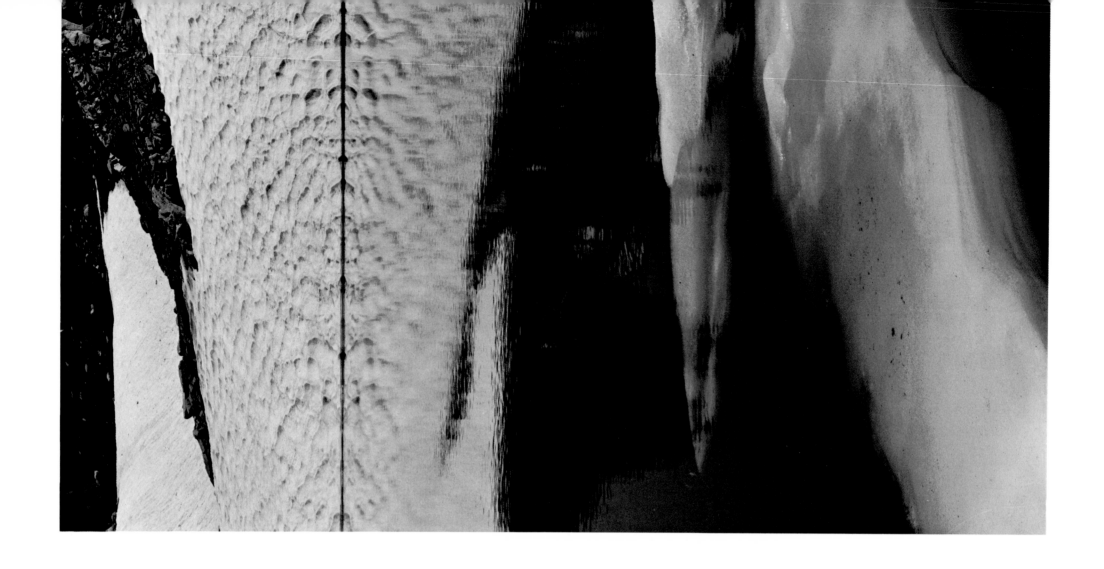

To know that light falls and fills, often without our knowing,
As an opaque vase fills to the brim from a quick pouring,
Fills and trembles at the edge yet does not flow over,
Still holding and feeding the stem of the contained flower.

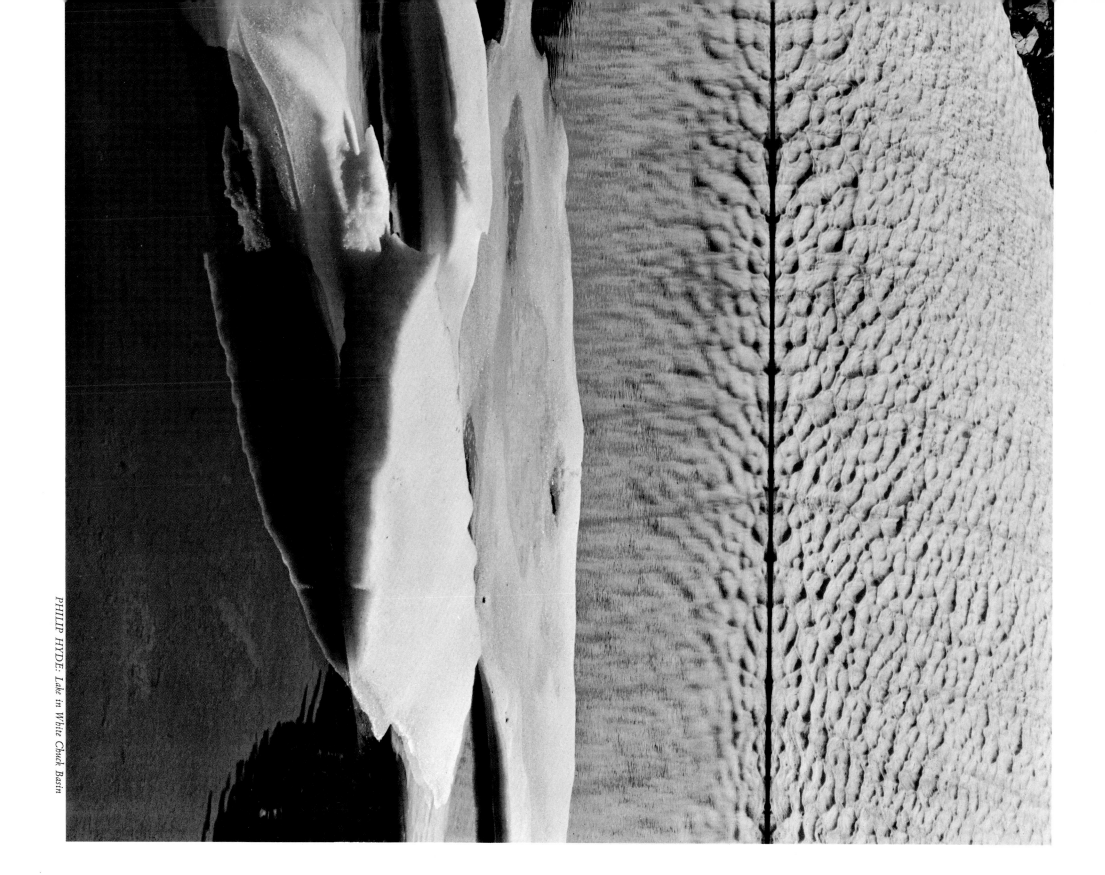

PHILIP HYDE: *Lake in White Chuck Basin*

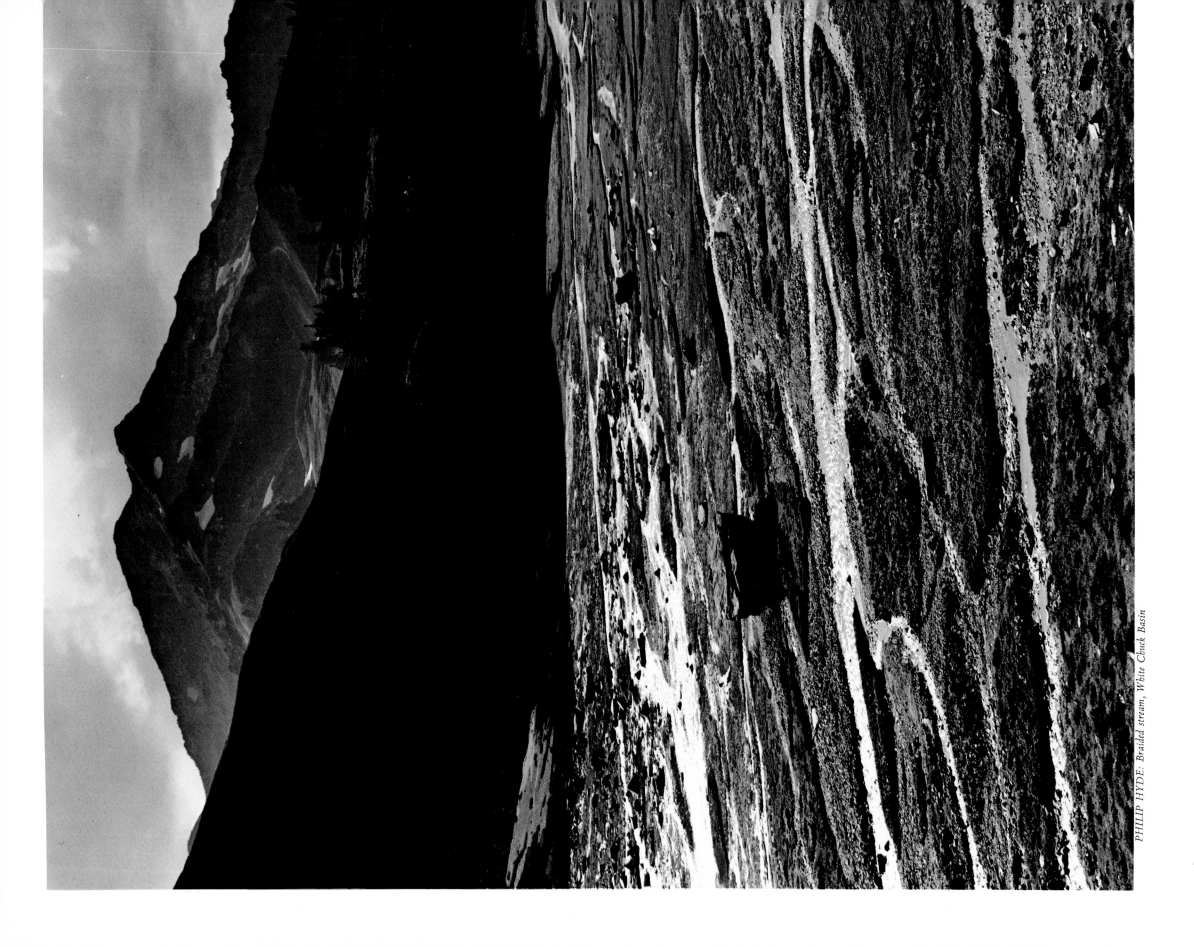

PHILIP HYDE: *Braided stream, White Chuck Basin*

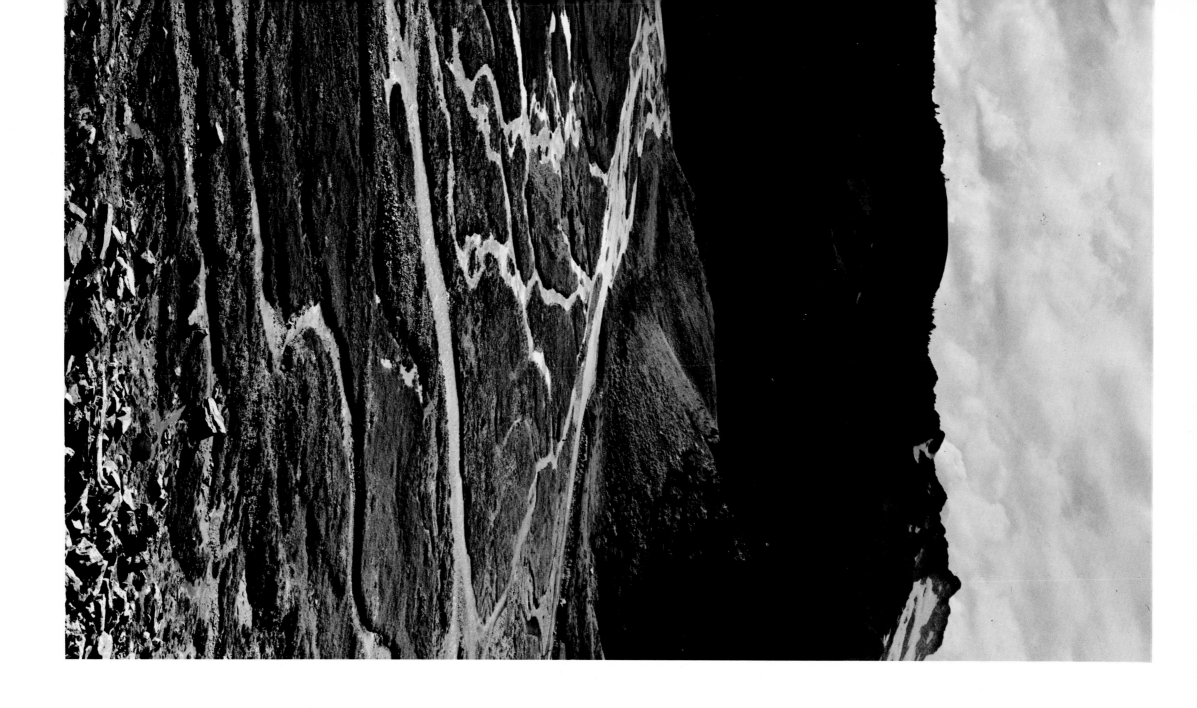

The sun declares the earth;
The stones leap in the stream;
On a wide plain, beyond
The far stretch of a dream,
A field breaks like the sea;
The wind's white with her name,
And I walk with the wind.

BOB and IRA SPRING: *Sunrise on lower slopes of Glacier Peak*

And I acknowledge my foolishness with God,
My desire for the peaks, the black ravines, the rolling mists
Changing with every twist of wind,
The unsinging fields where no lungs breathe,
Where light is stone.

Part 5

Rock and Ice

A T SOME STAGE in his North Cascades higher education, a student may feel called to one or another field of special interest, may find a genuine *vocation* (in the old definition with spiritual rather than economic meaning) as an expert in rock, ice, flowers, birds, rivers, or clouds.

A score or more professional scientists, sponsored partly or fully by universities or governmental agencies, currently pursue research in the North Cascades—classifying plants and measuring river flow and mapping rocks and investigating ecological relationships and studying long-range trends in the climate evidenced by fluctuations of glaciers. From the unique characteristics of this one mountain area they are adding new knowledge to man's total understanding of his world. Innumerable amateur scientists, as well, are learning things here they could not learn elsewhere, are enlarging their personal comprehension of the ways of nature—and not infrequently are bringing new data to the attention of the professionals.

Most students, though, choose the roving life of a dilettante, majoring in survey courses, learning a little about everything and not very much about anything.

At bottom are always rocks—though in actuality rocks cannot be the object of one's first course of North Cascades study, not when making a properly respectful entry through a valley forest. A professor of geology, then at the University of Washington but since moved to Texas, was once accused by his class of being unfriendly to vegetation, and replied that it was not so, that he was fond of greenery and favored having plenty of trees—as many as one to a square mile. With all due respect to this professor—whose recent elevation to membership in the National Academy of Science is small measure of his value to former students —it's not an impossibly long walk up above the trees to the high country where the bare bones of the mountains lie open to easy examination.

The most prominent structural features of the Cascades, the volcanoes, are the largest free-standing objects in the contiguous United States, a fact evident to anyone who has flown west across the nation and been impressed in flight by Rockies and Tetons, but near flight's end been staggered by the immense white piles along the Cascade crest.

The volcanoes are temporally dramatic, having happened a geologic instant ago. Much of the fun in walking around Glacier Peak comes from looking at the comparatively recent violence—layers of tuff sliced deep by the Suiattle and White Chuck Rivers, beds of pumice at Buck Creek Pass, bits of pumice littering summits many miles from Glacier—which 12,000 years ago cast ashes at least as far as Montana. And on a smaller scale, there is the Cinder Cone in the headwaters of the White Chuck, fragment of a toy volcano one can scramble up and down and all around in an hour.

However, the dominant geologic characteristic of the North Cascades is deformation and metamorphism. It is a range of rocks that have been fractured and splintered and mashed and compressed and dislocated, a range of giant faults and massive overthrusts, of myriad small faults and intrusions and contact zones, and all in all, at first reconnaisance, utter structural chaos. A single several-day walk may cross tuff, pumice, lava, granite, gneiss, schist, and breccia, and reveal a dozen other rocks with names familiar only to geologists, and another dozen only classifiable under a microscope. So varied are the metamorphic structures that the leading investigator of the subject, Professor Peter Misch of the University of Washington, once suggested the creation in the North Cascades of a "Metamorphism National Park," stating that in his experience—which extends from the Alps to the Himalaya—no other American range, and few in the world, are comparably complex.

The motion on a fault is exciting only to the informed eye (except during an earthquake), but little knowledge and imagination is needed to see and be impressed by the gouging done by glaciers ancient in man's measure, but recent in geologic time. Sometimes nakedly evident, and sometimes slightly disguised by a few millenia of falling rock, creeping soil, and rushing water, there are long deep glacier-cut troughs (that now occupied by Lake Chelan being the classic example), cirques and double cirques, step valleys and hanging valleys, cols and horns, polished-and-scratched slabs and streamlined *roches moutonées*, terminal moraines and lateral moraines, and all the other works of ice that make the North Cascades a rough country, and a steep, tall country from valley to summit.

Much of the same, of course, can be said of other Western American ranges. What distinguishes the North Cascades is that though the ancient glaciers have mostly melted away, here as elsewhere, new ones have been born in the centuries since the "climatic optimum" of two millenia ago, and many are currently thriving; some are advancing. To date, 519 living glaciers have been identified between Snoqualmie Pass and the Canadian border, covering 97.1 square miles—approximately triple the amount of glacier area in all the rest of the United States excluding Alaska.

There are steep valley glaciers, as on Glacier Peak, and flat valley glaciers, the South Cascade and the Klawati. There are wide apron glaciers such as the Redoubt and Inspiration. There are plateau glaciers, almost ice caps, like the Boston and White Chuck and Sulfide. There are complex glaciers like the Chickamin and Dana, the one flowing from upper névé into a valley tongue, and the other tumbling ice blocks over a cliff. There are hanging glaciers, as on the north wall of Goode and the east face of Fury, composed almost entirely of icefalls, and on a warm summer day rumbling constantly with avalanches. And by the hundred there are cirque glaciers, ranging down in size to the acres of ice tucked in a corner of White Rock Lakes.

And yet the proudest booster of the North Cascades would admit that all those 519 glaciers with all their 97.1 square miles would fit handily into a single Alaskan or Yukon superglacier, with plenty of room left over. The distinction of North Cascades ice is not so much its relative plenty as its context of meadows, streams, and forests —a context not common anywhere in the world, and especially not in the United States. It is, so to speak, *friendly ice* as compared to the Himalayan or Canadian Coast Range variety.

One can become a student of North Cascades ice in the forests of Milk Creek, at the point where the trail opens from shadowed greenery into a grassy flat with a view up to the shocking brilliance of the Ptarmigan Glacier. Or sitting amid the whistling marmots in Boston Basin, watching the avalanches on the north face of Johannesberg. Or, after spending a valley day in White Chuck forests, and a transition day in White Chuck meadows, strolling to the margin of the White Chuck Glacier, and perhaps even stepping a few safe yards out onto its blinding surface, in order to feel more deeply afterward the green of the grass below.

For grand glaciers that overpower mountains, there are Greenland and Antarctica. For glaciers that leave room for flowers and trees, and lakes and rivers—and people— there are the North Cascades.

High World

The Right Thing

Let others probe the mystery if they can.
Time-barried prisoners of Shall and Will—
The right thing happens to the happy man.

. . .

JOHN F. WARTH: *Magic Mountain from Doubtful Lake trail*

BOB and IRA SPRING: *Forbidden Peak*

The bird flies out, the bird flies back again;
The hill becomes the valley, and is still;
Let others delve that mystery if they can.

God bless the roots! — Body and soul are one!
The small become the great, the great the small;
The right thing happens to the happy man.

. . .

BOB and IRA SPRING: *Sunrise on lower slopes of Glacier Peak*

Child of the dark, he can out leap the sun,
His being single, and that being all;
The right thing happens to the happy man.

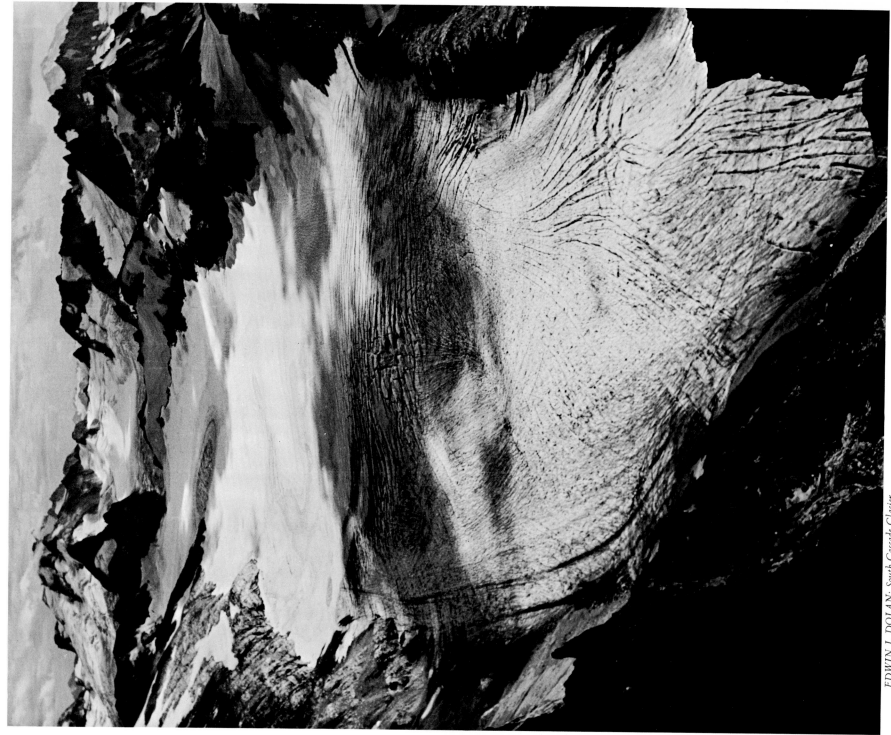

EDWIN J. DOLAN: *South Cascade Glacier*

Or he sits still, a solid figure when
The self-destructive shake the common wall;
Takes to himself what mystery he can,

. . . .

EDWIN J. DOLAN: *Icebergs   South Cascade Glacier*

BOB and IRA SPRING: Dome Peak

And praising change as the slow night comes on,
Wills what he would, surrendering his will
Till mystery is no more: No more he can.
The right thing happens to the happy man.

BOB and IRA SPRING: *Summit of Glacier Peak*

[67]

PHILIP HYDE: Sauk River forest

A breath is but a breath
And the smallest of our ties
With the long eternities,
And some men lie like trees,
The last to go is the bark,
The weathered, the tough outside.

Part 6

Green World

PERHAPS THE BEST introduction to the vegetable world begins in the mineral world of lifeless ice and rock; though no trip starts on a mountain top, many a traveler gains his passion for things that grow during the descent from such a summit as that of Glacier Peak. There is a fine simplicity in the functional architecture of the glaciers and cliffs two miles above the sea, yet after a long day amid the elemental purity of a line drawing, Appolonian man yields totally to Dionysian man at the first bright flower on the crest of a moraine, the first green moss in a creek below a snowfield. On the ascent there was the classicist's joy in rising from confusion into clarity; now on the descent there is the romantic's exuberance in diving into the clutter of meadow and tangle of forest, the rich seeming-chaos of life abundant.

Some North Cascades students specialize in trees and flowers, mosses and lichens and fungi, and find as much satisfaction in encountering species new to them as climbers do in attaining a summit, and are as excited by discovering a species new to the body of botanical knowledge as climbers are in making a first ascent.

Most students, though, are less systematic; through the years they come to recognize trees and flowers, and know them well, but it is a case of "I remember the face but not the name"—surely no bar to friendship. The dilettante's memories are not organized by species and family and measured dimensions, but are a grab-bag of moments in time when a tree (or a forest) or a flower (or a meadow) was intensely experienced.

Every traveler will sometime turn a corner in a trail and pass from trees merely large into a grove of Douglas fir absolutely huge, and at the hugest of all pause to circle the girth by eye, and look far up the straight trunk to the distant crown, and wonder whether this specimen is contemporary with Shakespeare, or perhaps Chaucer.

For many there will be *two*—and both times startled—discoveries of larch, the paradoxical "evergreen" that is not—first coming upon the tree in the spring, perhaps in dawn, when new-sprouting needles are a light, fresh green, and then in the autumn, perhaps in sunset, when the entire tree is a radiant yellow glow.

From west-side valleys one will have memories of individual hemlocks, with a delicacy of needles and cones and a limp softness of branches that seem inappropriate for a tree that grows so large, and from east-side valleys memories of Ponderosa pine, with a cinnamon gaudiness of bark pattern somehow suggestive of a great snake.

There may be a springtime evening, descending from a long climb, plunge-stepping and skating down the snow of a silver fir forest, when the trees pass by so swiftly that out of weariness comes a hypnotized awareness of more than individual whitish-barked trees, an awareness of all the trees merging together in a forest illumined not from the sky but by a soft inner light.

And one will question the prejudice against wild fire for the sake of the bleached snags of a silver forest, perhaps killed a century ago by a bolt of lightning and a sudden eruption of flame, but still standing upright as a reminder that wilderness—genuine wilderness—is the sum of many processes of life and death, growth and decay.

On a day of blue sky and cool wind, one may walk the narrow crest from Red Pass to White Mountain—the trench of the Sauk North Fork on the right, the headwaters of the White Chuck to the left—and with feet invisible under knee-high, wind-whipped flowers, feel the body gradually lose connection with solid ground and float weightlessly on a sea of color—color of forests below, color of flowers and sky all around.

On another bright and windy day one may climb Miner's Ridge through red heather, white heather, and yellow heather, all in fresh bloom, all mixed together, and the slope so steep that the red bells, the white bells, the yellow bells are only inches away from eyes and nose, and at length one seems not to be climbing upward on feet but swimming upward with hands and knees and elbows, affecting a butterfly stroke through a multi-colored froth of silent bells.

Or on a day of dense fog in the cirque of Pumice Creek, with no view except underfoot, one may on a single hillside count twenty-seven different flowers in bloom— most unknown by name but recognized from meadows of past years, but some never before separated out as individual components of mountain color.

For personal reasons that may or may not be known to the individual, each traveler develops favorites among flowers. The skunk cabbage with its garish yellow blossom and gross shiny leaves may come to have a poignance because it symbolizes the black ooze and green luxuriance of a subalpine meadow-marsh, remembered many a time as the prelude to higher meadows, and to glaciers and summits. Or perhaps one has a feeling for phlox because it is

an understated flower, a simple white sometimes tending into subtle blueness but never going all the way. Or moss campion because it grows in arid sands above the snow, the round clumps of tiny red blossoms dotting tiny green leaves startling against brown soil and gray rock. Or yellow stonecrop on a cliff, or fields of glacier lilies at the margin of a melting snowfield, or a smear of orange lichen on a frost-wedged flake of summit rock.

Even those who are color-blind learn by another sense to delight in one particular plant. Mountain thirst may be quenched with swallows of cold mountain water, and the quick ecstasy justifies thirst-building hours. There is a better way, though, a slower way, to quench a thirst— that of the alpine gourmet grazing on hands and knees in a field of blueberries, savoring tart squirts of juice from individual berries, then gathering a handful of fruit, letting anticipation build, and stuffing all into the mouth at once. When it is necessary to break off grazing, hoist pack, and continue on to camp or summit, the flavor lingers for hours and miles, and the stain on fingers, lips, and tongue remains for days, almost beyond memory of the berries.

The Manifestation

Many arrivals make us live: the tree becoming
Green, a bird tipping the topmost bough,
A seed pushing itself beyond itself,
The mole making its way through darkest ground,
The worm, intrepid scholar of the soil—
Do these analogies perplex? A sky with clouds,
The motion of the moon, and waves at play,
A sea-wind pausing in a summer tree.

What does what it should do needs nothing more.
The body moves, though slowly, toward desire.
We come to something without knowing why.

JOHN F. WARTH: *Buck Creek trail*

This urge, wrestle, resurrection of dry sticks,
Cut stems struggling to put down feet,
What saint strained so much,
Rose on such lopped limbs to new life?

I can bear underground, that sucking and sobbing,
In my veins, in my bones, I feel it, —
The small waters sweeping upward,
The tight grains parting at last.
When sprouts break out,
Slippery as fish,
I quail, lean to beginnings, sheath-out.

EDITH HARDIN ENGLISH: *Canadian dogwood*

JOHN F. WARTH: *Forest floor, western slope*

72

Wilderness Alps

In the Northern Cascades there is alpine wilderness that belongs to our national gallery. Such places are the last of our primeval landscapes, the few surviving samples of a natural world, to walk and rest in, to see, to listen to, to feel the mood of, to comprehend, to care about. There isn't much of it left. What there is is all all men will ever have, and all their children. It is only as safe as people, knowing about it, want it to be.

But do enough people know about it? We didn't, and went in to look it over. We had heard about the region, and about a conflict between those who wanted to use raw materials and those who wanted to preserve natural beauty. We weren't prepared for what began to unfold—an amazing wilderness of rugged alps built in grand scale, unique, unsurpassed anywhere in the United States.

JOHN WARTH, *Entiat River Road near end*

PHILIP HYDE. Suiattle River Valley from Miners Ridge

PHILIP HYDE. Head of Lake Chelan

74

JOHN WARTH. *Sulphur Creek Trail near Suiattle Road*

The Northern Cascades country was once, all of it, as wild as the sea—the wild, shining sea, shaping the earth through the ages, never the same, yet not to be changed by man, who long ago learned to accept it for what it is, even as we are now learning not to change some of the wild land, but to keep it natural, to seek from it answers to questions we may yet learn how to ask.

Can we set apart, unmanaged, unspoiled, enough of these places? Can we spare the stillness of a rain forest, where trees can live out their full span and return to the earth they came from? All that lives here repays in full for value received, nourishes as it has been nourished. Scores of centuries built this, a cool green world, hushed as a prayer. Man could wipe it out in a decade. Or consecrate it as a park, not to be impaired, a place where all generations could come to know the dignity of nature.

PHILIP HYDE. *Upper White Chuck Basin*

Our first trip in was a flight—too hurried, too cut off, too unreal for us to feel the country or remember the shape of the waves of the storm-tossed sea of peaks. We knew it was great country, big country. We also saw that its size alone could not protect it. On the west side men were already clearcutting the last virgin forests, getting timber and pulp from forested avenues of approach needed very much as primeval setting and living space to look at and to look from. Crossing Cascade Pass, in the heart of the wilderness, we were but a few minutes from other wild forests, also wanted for their timber, but needed as setting too.

PHILIP HYDE. *Lake near Heather Pass*

PHILIP HYDE. *Chiwawa Mountain and meadow above Lyman Lake*

PHILIP HYDE. Ten Peak Range and meadows above Image Lake

PHILIP HYDE. Sierra Club Camp at White Pass, Sloan Peak

Our trail climbed grassy canyonsides to a small shelter in its own private alp below the pass. We only had time that day to explore a lower side trail for a mile or two, to see what a wilderness forest is like when man leaves it to its own wondrous devices. We walked waist-deep in ferns, quietly, looking backward on the eternity that has made this forest what it is. We poked along the high trails, wandered through the grass-lands, let the mountain wind blow away flat-land cares.

JOHN WARTH: Spring part way up Green Mountain

PHILIP HYDE. Slopes of Sahale Arm, near Cascade Pass

PHILIP HYDE. White Chuck Glacier

PHILIP HYDE. Snow tunnel, Washington Pass

DAVID R. SIMONS. *Image Lake and Glacier Peak at sunrise*

Almost everybody got out on a glacier, too. And we kept looking for a hole in the mist through which to glimpse the monarch of this country, Glacier Peak. We watched the cloud cap, the strange lenticular cloud that the wind blows through, leaving the cloud there.

PHILIP HYDE. *Glacier Peak from ridge above Lake Ann*

Everywhere there were wild gardens. And here, deep in the heart of the little-known alps, seemingly remote, we met at noon a friend who had left New York City late the night before, a whole continent away.

PHILIP HYDE: *Lake Ann from trail to Heather Pass*

PHILIP HYDE. Liberty Bell, Early Winters Creek

PHILIP HYDE. *Sierra Club campfire, Washington Pass*

He came up through virgin forest with huge trees, almost a rain forest, still as a cathedral, in it a clear stream from an unscarred watershed, clear in spite of the northern weather. The northern traveler, we all knew, is seldom bored by blue skies. But then, monotonous fair weather can't build mountains like these, and their glaciers and forests and flowers. We liked the way the mountains looked and discovered how to like what made them that way—don't scurry for cover and miss the show. Stay out and be part of it! Not on a high peak, of course. But take a walk, down in the sheltered valley. So we walked out into it, heads up, and felt the freshness the rains bring, saw new patterns, smelled the wet leaves, now washed and cool, and we looked up to see the old contest between the crags and the mists.

We were close to the pass, making camp, our own mountain world spread out around us, each clump of trees a timberline penthouse, each room perfectly air-conditioned. Then dawn brought a flush to Glacier Peak.

JOHN WARTH. *Glacier Peak from Green Mountain*

The sun would light all this mountain land soon, and we hope it will always reveal wilderness there—in the avenues of unspoiled forest, in the flashing waters of the sidestreams and the river, in the friendly lower gardens and grassy alplands, up at timberline and in tundra, on the glaciers and peaks.

Other people will want to be walking our trails, up where the tree reaches high for the cloud, up where the flower takes the summer wind with beauty, and the summer rain too. They will want to discover for themselves the wildness that the ages have made perfect.

They have a right to discover wild places. They can discover them, but only if we keep some wildness in between the shining seas; only if man remembers, in his rising tide, not to engulf his last islands of wilderness.

[Text adapted from the film, "Wilderness Alps of Stehekin."]

I saw a body dancing in the wind,
A shape called up out of my natural mind;
I heard a bird stir in its true confine;
A nestling sighed—I called that nestling mine;
A partridge drummed; a minnow nudged its stone; . . .

Part 7

Other Creatures

STUFFED IN MUSEUMS, caged in zoos, roasted in ovens, surrounded by whirring and clicking cameras on national park highways, trapped in the cross-hairs of rifles during hunting season, the other creatures of earth are the constant object of man's lively interest. No matter how jaded one may be with the bathos of Bambi-ism, meeting an animal in its wilderness home—any animal, however commonplace—gives perspective on the place of man in the wilderness, and in the civilized world.

Sad to say, it is not easy any more to gain a wide ac-quaintance among the original residents of the North Cascades. The wolf apparently is extinct, or next to it, and the cougar so rare that many a lifelong traveler of the range has never heard a scream or seen a track. The bear, also legally classified as a bad citizen, has virtually disap-peared from some areas, and the coyote survives only be-cause man has not yet devised a practical method of total extermination. It is claimed that the mountain goat popu-lation is being held constant (for its own good), only the "surplus" harvested, and this may be true, but surely the new generations of goats have learned to be distrustful since trophy hunting resumed in 1948. Though protected by law, not even the marmot is safe, since many hunters consider him an alpine fink, warning away deer with his whistle. And the annual potshooters' toll of chipmunks and squirrels (and trail signs) is beyond estimation.

More often than not, one encounters animals as unseen presences—finding tracks or sign along a trail, or an aban-doned nest of dry grass under a rock, or tooth marks in a riverside willow, or tufts of goat wool caught in the heather—or perhaps lying in a sleeping bag in the total black of a cedar grove at Nightmare Camp on Lightning Creek, listening to thuds out beyond flashlight range, and reciting the old Scottish prayer that asks deliverance

"from ghosties and ghoulies, long-leggitty beasties, and things that go bump in the night."

Occasionally a traveler observes creatures of the wilder-ness, other than the omnipresent deer and chipmunk, in their natural condition, and is even accepted by them as a fellow citizen, or at least as part of the landscape.

One may sit quietly for an hour or more in the upper-most meadow of Mixup Arm, until the large family of marmots living in the frost-wedged castle a few yards be-low poke their noses out from various caves, one by one, the oldsters pretending not to see the visitor so long as he stays put, the youngsters, only half-grown and still baby-faced, crowding and shoving and climbing over each other to get a better look.

Or in a springtime forest on the slopes of Mount Pugh one may hear a scratching noise above, and look up to a pair of bear cubs clinging to a tree trunk—and glance quickly around to see if their mother is in sight, feeling eerily certain of being within *her* sight.

Or on a rockslide near Lake Anne one may chance upon a silent life-and-death drama, a single pika closely pur-sued by two weasels, all three dodging swiftly in and out among granite boulders below the hiker's feet, unaware of the human presence, the pursuers solely concerned with catching supper, the pursued with avoiding that particu-lar supper.

Or one may lie in a sleeping bag at Many Waterfalls Camp, snatching packs and boots and food supplies to safety within the human circle, daring to take no offensive action against the porcupine which is determined to find the meal that somewhere here is to be had.

With birds as with flowers a traveler may learn only a few names and still know many individuals, and some among them special favorites. The dipper *is* the river, as the long trilling call of the varied thrush *is* the loneliness and deep repose of the dawn forest. In meadows one may remember ptarmigan chicks ignoring their mother's clucks and wandering in and out of camp, periodically exploding underfoot; in cliffs, a hummingbird nearly scaring a climber from his handholds by darting at his red stocking cap, mistaken for the Promised Blossom; on a summit, a distant hawk or eagle whose point of motion stresses how much air there is in the valley and sky.

And other things than birds have wings: into every North Cascades lifetime comes, more than once, a trial by mosquitoes, with moments of despair, as when trapped in a tangle of slide alder, and moments of restrained fury when one sits in a meadow and kills, and kills, and kills, and perhaps even interludes of maniac sadism when one does not kill but grasps individual mosquitoes gently, pulls off their hypodermics, and releases them to fly again but nevermore drink blood.

Mosquitoes seem an impersonal force of nature, relentless as sunshine on a south slope but equally unaware of themselves and their victims. Not so flies, for flies have sharp eyes and hyperactive brains, and the obscene malice of their ugly faces and arrogant buzzing is intensely personal. Now and then there will come a summer week of hot, humid, airless days that breed flies by the million and stir them to lunatic fits, days when wives weep and children learn their fathers are not omnipotent, and when a hiker may come to a river and in desperation plunge his head under the surface for respite, and once within the cold biteless water seriously consider never coming out again.

However, most North Cascades bugs are good neighbors, and interesting to students who learn to focus small. Crossing a snowfield, one may suddenly observe it's not all sterile ice, but is crowded with beetles and other creeping creatures. And perhaps one will discover with nausea, taking a second look at a half-eaten snowball, that ice worms are not a droll legend.

Sometimes one may glimpse a cobweb high in the sky, caught momentarily in the sun, airship of a most improbable flier, a spider become for some reason restless and thus building a web, cutting it loose in the wind, and trusting chance to find him a new home—a reckless way to travel, but not beyond the admiration of those who walk high hills.

I hear the owls, the soft callers, coming down from the hemlocks.
The bats weave in and out of the willows,
Wing-crooked and sure,
Downward and upward,
Dipping and veering close to the motionless water.

ROBERT E. FRENKEL: *Trout Lake, Alpine Lakes wilderness*

DAVID SIMONS: *Agnes Gorge*

The river turns on itself,
The tree retreats into its own shadow.
I feel a weightless change, a moving forward
As of water quickening before a narrowing channel
When banks converge, and the wide river whitens;
Or when two rivers combine, the blue glacial torrent
And the yellowish-green from the mountainy upland, —
At first a swift rippling between rocks,
Then a long running over flat stones . . . .

Part 8

Summer Day

THE IDEAL North Cascades day is one of bright sun (but with gusts of cool wind) and blue sky (but with a few harmless and picturesque cumulus clouds scattered around). Numerous as such days are, they are out-numbered by days in one way or another less than ideal, and those who sit in the city waiting for perfection may sit out the entire summer, year after year. And so, though it's the rare traveler who deliberately sets out along a trail in the face of a hopeless forecast, any traveler, if he is ever to see the high country, must take chances. And actually some of the supreme North Cascades experiences —in retrospect at least—have to do with times when the luck is bad and one is caught in a storm.

A walker may arrive alone at Image Lake in a July blizzard and hole up in the lean-to during a day of snow and wind, and a night of the same, and another morning, and have every expectation of another similar afternoon and night and day.

Awakened at noon by a brightness and a quietness, he may sluggishly stumble into fog for a bit of exercise before the snow resumes, and the hibernation. Along the trail to Lady Camp Basin the fog lifts from the ground and separates into billows moving east; between them he glimpses scraps of blue—blue so intense after long sleep and gray-ness as to be frightening, for what *is* it, asks his sleep-dazed mind, that makes the sky blue?

The green grass sweeping up into white clouds and blue sky seems oddly disconnected from the green grass falling into far-off forests of the Suiattle, and the hiker, still only half-awake, teeters back and forth on the narrow trail, trying to rationalize the tilted horizon which has one edge in the river and the other in the sky, nothing anywhere secure and stable for his eye to balance against, no horizontal and no vertical, everything in a whirl. The clouds rise steadily, and for reasons not known so does he, and approaching the summit of Plummer he comes very near the billows, which sometimes dip down unpredictably and swallow him in rushing whiteness; the meadow seems to lean outward over the Suiattle valley of air, and the heather he grips in both hands is a tenuous connection to the steepening wall, almost a ceiling.

On the summit he slowly stands erect, surrounded by cloud and air and sky, held to earth merely by the friction of his boots; the motion of the clouds seems to be the motion of the earth turning on its axis and he has the irrational fear that from lack of lubrication or a bit of sand in the gears the spin might stutter briefly, flinging him off the peak of Plummer east over Cloudy Pass and Lake Chelan and onward through space to wherever the clouds are going in their orbit.

Eventually Glacier Peak emerges across the Suiattle to the south, and Dome Peak across Canyon Creek to the north, and they solidly anchor the horizon. The clouds begin to burn away in sunset, turning a peculiar shimmering brown, then orange and scarlet, then dwindling to pink wisps that dissolve into the evening sky. Descending to Image Lake along the crest of Miner's Ridge, the hiker knows that tomorrow there will be a clear dawn and a hot afternoon, and toward evening other hikers will arrive in the high country, and he wishes them well but pities them for missing the storm and the hours that followed.

Everyone enjoys the end of a storm and some enjoy the storm itself—some, but not all.

On the Labor Day weekend of 1964 a party camped on the slopes of Hidden Lake Peak awoke in the morning to the sound of flapping tarp and spattering hail, and after a long, watchful breakfast in the sleeping bags decided this was no passing cumulonimbus squall but a serious front, possibly even the beginning of a genuine three-day blow. However, the road was only a few miles distant, downhill the Cascade River, may sleep every night under the pitter-patter of rain on the tarp and hike through drizzle to Boston Basin, Cascade Pass, Sahale Arm, and Cache Col, and never see anything but wet meadow and cold snow underfoot, and gray cloud around and occasional brightness off to the east.

Other times clouds may envelop the entire main range, forcing a retreat farther east, all the way east of Lake Chelan, into country quite unlike any other in the North Cascades, and to a student of Wordsworth and Smythe reminiscent of Snowdon in Wales and Ben Nevis in Scotland. The peaks of Safety Harbor Creek, Prince Creek, Fish Creek, and War Creek are high, extending well above 8,000 feet, but the meadows are also high, and broad, and gentle. The glaciers never worked here long enough for deep dissection and left a biscuit-board topography of shallow cirques and short cliffs; succeeding millenia of mass-wasting have added stable talus and rolling felsenmeer; what remains now is a large open highland allowing easy roaming from basin bottom to peak top.

One may sometimes walk these meadows in sunshine under scraps of fuzzy-edged clouds which quit raining an hour ago and now are vanishing, and look down and *down* 7,000 feet to Lake Chelan (and only from here can one see how narrow is the water road and how deep is the trench) and look across the trench (and only from here can one see how immensely wide it is) and off to the west see clouds that perhaps are not storming but surely are wetting down the entire crest with good-weather rain.

all the way; there was no panic, and retreat was orderly. Traversing the meadows above Sibley Creek the guide pointed out to his youngest client, a five-year-old girl, the wonder of a summer snowstorm whitening the heather around and the dimly seen cliffs above, and the magic of snowflakes caught in her mittens and eyelashes, and the drama of the black clouds over the Cascade River, with a sunburst breaking between to spotlight rain sheeting from a cloud bottom into the valley bottom. When a fresh fury of a squall drove up Sibley Creek, the guide commented on how delightful was the wind in her eyes, the sleet on her cheeks, and how gaily her sisters, ten and eleven years old, were laughing and dancing down the switchbacks below, their shrieks of glee reaching up between loud gusts. To all of which the client at last replied, "I *hate* it!"

In all frankness, even the most sanctimonious of North Cascades Pollyannas sometimes feel not quite up to the joys of another storm, and sneak across into the rain shadow, using the Cascade crest as a buffer against moist ocean air.

Some summers, or portions of some summers, the escape to the rain shadow turns out to be a most artful dodge. A party may spend days camped in the headwaters of the Stehekin River, sleeping every night under stars and hiking each day to the edge of "good-weather" clouds filling the west-side valleys and pushing fingers of fog over the crest—fog that melts in the east-side air above Doubtful Lake and Pelton Lake and Horseshoe Basin. Another party, camped during these same days in the headwaters of

The sun! The sun! And all we can become!
And the time ripe for running to the moon!
In the long fields, I leave my father's eye;
And shake the secrets from my deepest bones;
My spirit rises with the rising wind;
I'm thick with leaves and tender as a dove,
I take the liberties a short life permits—
I seek my own meekness;
I recover my tenderness by long looking.
By midnight I love everything alive.
Who took the darkness from the air?
I'm wet with another life.
Yea, I have gone and stayed.

JOHN F. WARTH: *Douglas Glacier, Mount Logan, from Fisher Creek*

The Way It Was

Lake Chelan (stereo)

[The late Hugh Courtney, homesteader in Stehekin Valley, let us look through his collection of early-day photographs and lent us many of them, making it possible for us to assemble this six-page album of the work of various photographers, most of them now unknown. We include two stereo pairs, which may be viewed in three- dimensions without artificial aid—by a patient man. Place the book on the floor, well illuminated, and look at a pencil tip held about one-third the distance from your eyes to the book. Without tilting your head or changing the slightly crossed alignment of your eyes, forget about the pencil and think about Lake Chelan, which will suddenly acquire new depth.]

Belle of Chelan, built in 1908

The stern-wheeler

Campbell Hotel, Chelan, built 1898

Stern-wheeler

Hotel Field (Cheney), Stehekin

Recreation at Moore's, up-lake

Clearing Crew for the Railroad Creek railroad, 1899. Photograph by J. R. Moore

JOHN F. WARTH: *Moss-covered shea near Sulphur Creek campground*

PHOTOGRAPHER UNKNOWN: *The Lake* (stereo)

ROBERT F. FRENKEL: *Floating ice, Doubtful Lake*

Was I too glib about eternal things,
An intimate of air and all its songs?

Part 9

Primal World

A MISTAKEN NOTION, commonly advanced by those who would "open up the country to the people," is that there is a single sort of wilderness experience —strenuous and perilous—and a single sort of wilderness traveler—heavily muscled, highly skilled, and fearless to the point of foolhardiness. In point of fact, the wilderness of the North Cascades is a mixture of many different terrains ranging from difficult to easy, and its visitors have widely assorted goals, abilities, and travel tactics. There are many varieties of wilderness experience, and no absolute calculus by which one can be ranked above another, except in the degree of genuine wildness, as measured by freedom from the sights and sounds of machinery and sheep and other gross intrusions of civilization, and by the unrestricted, uninterrupted continuity of nature and its processes.

The size of a wilderness is a prime determinant of how wild it really is—how many days one can travel inward from an edge before beginning to emerge on the other side. For some North Cascades travelers, the magnitude of the existing wilderness is its greatest attraction, and they find their highest pleasure in long trail walks, many days long, such as two days up Thunder Creek to Park Creek Pass and then another day down Park Creek to the Stehekin River, or two days up the Suiattle River to Suiattle Pass and Cloudy Pass and another day down through Lyman Basin and along Railroad Creek to Holden, or a minimum five-day loop starting at the abandoned Trinity Mine, going up Phelps Creek to Spider Pass, down into Lyman Basin, up to Cloudy Pass, down to Miners' Creek, up to Middle Ridge and Buck Creek Pass, and down Buck Creek to Trinity again. On these and innumerable similar trail hikes, some straight across the wilderness from one boundary to another, some winding and circling through the interior, one can spend days at a time in lands where the trail itself is virtually the only modification of the primeval condition of the land.

The roughness of a wilderness also determines how wild it is, and for some this is the prime value of the North Cascades—the opportunity for the sort of trip called a semiexpedition because in everything but duration it resembles full-scale expeditions, with several days needed to reach the objective and several more to get back, with a route that goes beyond trails, perhaps through brush and across un-bridged rivers, perhaps over glaciers and cliffs, and perhaps all these. No party has yet reached Bear Lake in less than three days, whether from Hannegan Pass and the Chilliwack, or the Little Beaver and Whatcom Pass, or Perry Creek and the Redoubt Glacier, and that's why it's so much worth reaching, and why so few ever have. One variant of the famous Ptarmigan Traverse goes south from Cascade Pass up the Cache Glacier to Cache Col, down to Kool-Aid Lake, over the Red Ledge to the Middle Cascade Glacier, up to the Spider-Formidable Col, around the headwaters of Flat Creek to Yang Yang Lakes, up the LeConte Glacier, down to the South Cascade Glacier, down to White Rock Lakes, across the Dana Glacier and over a spur of Dome Peak to the Chickamin Glacier, around a spur of Blue Mountain to Blue Lake, along the Hanging Gardens to Canyon Lake and to Image Lake, and down to the Suiattle River—half a dozen alpine cols, half a dozen glaciers, no trail between the Cache Glacier and Canyon Lake, and for even a rather strong party enjoying perfect weather, and taking no time out for climbing, rest, or side explorations, requiring between five and seven days of steady travel, above timberline all the way.

For some a major dimension of North Cascades wildness is the vertical—the steep rise from valley forests through meadows and moraines and cliff and ice to the culminating summits. Fine country it is, surely, for climbing, or more properly, wilderness mountaineering, since here a climber needs not only the skills of rock and ice, but also those of trail walking, camping, backpacking, river fording, brush fighting, avalanche predicting, weather guessing, and cross-country navigating—not perhaps on any single trip, but certainly during a season devoted to reaching summits deep in the back country. Though the Golden Age of North Cascades climbing ended some years ago, with all the large peaks climbed by their easiest routes, the Silver Age of making first ascents of satellite peaks and placing new routes on the great walls is just well underway. No party has yet attempted the legendary overhang of Bear Mountain, perhaps because several days are needed merely to reach the base; Bonanza Peak, at 9,511 feet the highest nonvolcanic peak in the entire Cascade Range from California into Canada, has virgin walls that have not yet even been looked at carefully by parties capable of attempting them. For years to come climbers will be finding new routes in the vertical wilderness of the North Cascades, as well as repeating the old ones, easy and difficult.

The width and height and roughness of the North Cascades wilderness challenge some trail walkers, semi-expeditioners, and climbers to travel fast and far and long, testing their strength and ability near the absolute limit, for the sake of covering as much ground as possible within the time available. Such marathons may seem a disrespectful, even a wasteful, use of the wilderness, there being no leisure to linger over waterfalls and flowers, yet the very speed of passage has a value, compressing waterfalls and flowers and trees and rocks and glaciers and lakes and sunrises and sunsets and fogs and good-weather rains into a unified wilderness impression. And possibly one of the closest approaches to the mystic experience sought by the transcendentalists comes during a rest stop near the end of an eighteen-hour day, the body anesthetized by fatigue, the consciousness released from flesh and seemingly without intermediary of sense organs entering directly into the sky, or the river, or the forest.

However, among North Cascades travelers there are reformed marathoners who once were made neurotic by rest stops that lasted beyond the statutory five minutes, by rates of climb that fell below the established minimum rate of 1,000 feet per hour, by trips that did not culminate in a summit register—travelers who now feel, to misquote Water Rat in *The Wind in the Willows*, that "there is *nothing*—absolutely nothing—half so much worth doing as simply messing about in moraines." They may still climb peaks when convenient, but only incidental to subtler

goals. As they once bagged summits, now they bag cirques and cols, rivers and forests. Having climbed Goode and Logan and enjoyed looking down into the North Fork of Bridge Creek, now they hike up the valley floor of the North Fork of Bridge Creek and enjoy looking up the hanging glaciers to the summits of Goode and Logan. Having climbed Glacier Peak and enjoyed looking down the long flanks of ice to the meadows and trees, they now enjoy seeing the ice beyond a foreground of trees and meadows. As climbers they sought to know mountains by reaching their summits; now they seek to know the same mountains better by reaching their bottoms. It's the same mountain, seen from the top, seen from the bottom, seen from across the valley, seen in spring, autumn, sunshine, and storm, yet every view is a new experience, a new dimension.

But what of the traveler who for reasons of age or illness or inexperience cannot probe deeply into the wilderness? There still remain, anachronisms though they are, road-boomers whose love affair with the automobile is as passionate now as in 1910, and who wish the wilderness to be made easily available to all, including the very young and very old, the ill, the inexperienced, and the lazy. However, no one ever knows wilderness riding in an automobile, and the road that opens up wilderness also destroys it. On the other hand, there is such a thing as vicarious pleasure in wilderness—walking a mile beyond the threshold, or perhaps merely sitting on the boundary and looking in, and from the visible wildness sensing the magnificence of the unseen—a magnificence that would be lost in noise and fumes if it all could be seen from the window of an automobile.

Some travelers go deep, high, and fast into North Cascades wilderness, others make slow and shallow penetrations. Some go by foot, some by horse. Some go in conducted outings, so they may learn from skilled companions, and some go in small groups of congenial friends, and some go alone, in the way of Thoreau and Muir. Some go for a weekend, some for a summer, and some once and some repeatedly throughout their lives. Some go young, some old. And some stand on the edge and marvel.

There are many varieties of wilderness experience, and North Cascades travelers may argue among themselves which is the best. However, all agree that this is a wilderness which must be preserved undiminished and fully natural, for their sakes and for those of their children and great-grandchildren, and for all others who seek occasional refuge from the pressures of a steadily more raucous civilization.

A Light Breather

The spirit moves,
Yet stays:
Stirs as a blossom stirs,
Still wet from its bud-sheath,
Slowly unfolding,
Turning in the light with its tendrils;
Plays as a minnow plays,
Tethered to a limp weed, swinging,
Tail around, nosing in and out of the current,
Its shadows loose, a watery finger;
Moves, like the snail,
Still inward,
Taking and embracing its surroundings,
Never wishing itself away,
Unafraid of what it is,
A music in a hood,
A small thing,
Singing.

PHILIP HYDE: Forest floor, Sauk River

ROBERT F. FRENKEL: *Glacier Peak from Alpine Lakes "Limited Area." Patch-cutting on Tonga Ridge, 1959*

Moss-Gathering

To loosen with all ten fingers held wide and limber
And lift up a patch, dark-green, the kind for lining cemetery baskets,
Thick and cushiony, like an old-fashioned doormat,
The crumbling small hollow sticks on the underside mixed with roots,
And wintergreen berries and leaves still stuck to the top, —
That was moss-gathering.
But something always went out of me when I dug loose those carpets
Of green, or plunged to my elbows in the spongy yellowish moss of
the marshes:
And afterwards I always felt mean, jogging back over the logging road,
As if I had broken the natural order of things in that swampland;
Disturbed some rhythm, old and of vast importance,
By pulling off flesh from the living plant;
As if I had committed, against the whole scheme of life, a desecration.

JOHN F. WARTH: *Eldorado and foreground; ". . . actually, it is multiple-use logging," the photographer explains; "the logging gash is obscured by the tree."*

Part 10

Nibbling

DANIEL BOONE is quoted as having said, in regard to proper behavior in a wilderness, "If you aren't sure of the right thing to do, don't do anything." On the whole Boone's philosophy is a pretty good rule of thumb. A traveler lost in wilderness is much better off sitting still and letting others find him than striking blindly off in any random direction and getting more thoroughly lost. And nations of today, when pondering how best to use their small remaining portions of wilderness, are much wiser to let them alone than to tinker thoughtlessly with nature's management. For all the power of its rivers and storms, the immensity of its peaks and the ancience of its forests, wilderness is a delicate and dynamic balance between many forces, including a natural succession of forms of life; the balance is all too easily upset and the wilderness destroyed.

That the heartland of the North Cascades should be for the most part let alone has been evident to generations of travelers. As long ago as 1906 a national park was first proposed in the North Cascades, by the Mazamas, and in 1917, describing in *Cosmopolitan Magazine* her pack-train journey from Lake Chelan to Lyman Basin, down the Agnes to the Stehekin, and over Cascade Pass and down the Cascade River to Marblemount, Mary Roberts Rinehart felt comfortably certain that a park would be created by the following summer. In 1937 a special committee of the National Park Service reported that "the area is unquestionably of national park caliber, is more valuable used as such than for any other use now ascertainable, and should receive park status under the National Park Service as the agency set up for providing highest conservational use and protection . . . will outrank in its scenic, recreational, and wildlife values any existing national park and any other possibility for such a park within the United States."

Twice a North Cascades National Park has seemed a near possibility, once in the early years of the national park concept, and again in the 1930's. Now the movement for a park is again underway, and the national awareness of the need is more intense than ever—as it must be, for this is the last chance. The tinkerers, the spoilers, are abroad in the range, and if the existing plans of the United States Forest Service for multiple-use exploitation of public lands are allowed to be carried out, Americans will lose their finest opportunity for a wilderness parkland—and they will lose it soon, and in fact are losing it now in annual nibbles.

What *is* wilderness? Wilderness is what now exists in the center of the North Cascades—a large geographic province where the intricately intermingled processes of nature continue without major human interruption.

What *is* "multiple use?" Multiple use is what now is moving inward toward that center—the doctrine that Forest Service land managers can produce a cornucopia of economic and recreational riches without disrupting the natural balance or reducing the wild beauty.

As has been observed, both wilderness preservation and multiple-use development are for many of their respective proponents matters of faith, beyond the realm of rational discussion. However, even among the true believers on both sides, the argument in the North Cascades is not between wilderness and multiple use, but between how much of each, and where. It is the opinion here that the Forest Service is extending multiple-use development into areas that should be managed primarily for protection of the scenery, and also into areas that should be let completely alone, left for nature to manage.

To see Forest Service nibbling in progress, one can drive to the end of the White Chuck River road, now within six miles of Kennedy Hot Springs, at the base of Glacier Peak, and planned eventually to go all the way, sprouting tributaries on both sides of the valley. From the end of the road one can see the near, bright ice of Glacier Peak—across a foreground of stumps. And to see the system of side-roads developing, one can drive above the White Chuck on the Meadow Mountain complex linking logging patches together—with all the intervening trees, publicly owned trees, to go in their turn.

From the Cascade River one can see stumps and second growth along the road and across the valley, and turn aside to visit the stumplands—publicly owned stumplands—of Sibley Creek, a mile from the meadows, and of Marble Creek, with the glaciered wall of Eldorado above.

Voyaging up Lake Chelan in the *Lady of the Lake*, one can often see fresh-cut logs floating beside the Lucerne dock, part of the annual cut in Railroad Creek—second only to the Stehekin as a way into wilderness from the water road. And despite the personal promises of current officials—promises with absolutely no statutory guarantee—under Forest Service management further logging is also ultimately inevitable in the Stehekin itself, and eventually in such major tributary valleys as the lower portion of Agnes Creek and in Bridge Creek.

From the Suiattle River road one can drive into the logging show underway high on Green Mountain, and look up and down the valley, and across the valley, over miles of temporary trees, and one can walk up the Sulphur Creek and Downey Creek trails through miles of doomed forests. And it's all public land.

Logging either has been done or is in progress or is indicated as eventually coming, on published Forest Service plans and road-engineering maps, in the lower portions of Newhalem Creek, Illabot Creek, Found Creek, Roush Creek, Sonny Boy Creek, Kindy Creek, Buck Creek, Lime Creek, Elliot Creek, Sloan Creek, Bedal Creek, Cadet Creek, Panther Creek, Phelps Creek, Falls Creek, the Sauk River, and the North Fork of the Entiat River—corridors of forest leading to meadows and peaks, corridors fast being converted from wilderness into "tree farms," being subtracted bit by bit from the central scenic climax. Not all of these valleys are yet logged, but all are doomed.

One can drive to the farthest west-side extension of the North Cross-State Highway near Ross Lake, or the farthest east-side extension near Washington Pass, and see wilderness vanishing not in nibbles but in gulps as logging proceeds along Early Winters Creek and creeps into the enormous valley of Thunder Creek—one of the supreme North Cascades valleys, connecting at Park Creek Pass with Stehekin drainage, and carrying meltwater from some

of the largest glaciers in the range. As for State Creek, Granite Creek, and Ruby Creek—along which the future highway will run—the Forest Service officials currently responsible for these valleys have made personal promises that logging will be for the most part limited to whatever is required for purposes of controlling disease and ensuring public safety and convenience. However, these promises are purely personal, and in no way bind future officials, and therefore are no longe-range protection at all. Many students of public policy question whether this highway should ever have been allowed to emerge from the cocoon of small-town boosterism. Be that as it may, the road is too far along to stop, or to divert to a wiser route—but the decision still remains as to whether it will become an artery of multiple-use logging, mining, dude-ranching, hamburger-frying, and curio-purveying, or else a North Cascades Parkway.

One can climb to the meadows of Pumice Creek cirque and look out down the White Chuck, and see how the unit of wilderness forest and wilderness peaks is being chopped apart, and realize with horror that there is no statutory guarantee that the sounds of bulldozer and chainsaw will not reach even here, on the slopes of Glacier Peak itself, with logging extending up Kennedy Ridge to within an hour's stroll of the heather. The current Forest Service plan for the White Chuck envisions a road to Kennedy Hot Springs (for "recreation only"—poor solace where there should be no road for any purpose) but does not forbid logging if it is, in the opinion of the Forest Supervisor, compatible with recreation. It is good to know that the incumbent Supervisor has no plans to log Kennedy Ridge. However, it is less reassuring to realize that he will someday have a successor who might very well resemble his immediate predecessor, a man who urged upon others his view that neatly logged slopes supporting vigorous stands of second-growth timber are a genuine scenic asset.

One can hike nine miles up the Downey Creek trail to its end, and then climb thousands of feet through brush and forest and meadow, and after several days of respectful approach sit on a peak above White Rock Lakes and look out southwest along Downey Creek and see logging scars along the Suiattle and on Green Mountain, and visualize future logging in Downey Creek itself. And look out northwest down the South Cascade Glacier and see logging coming around the corner from the Cascade River and surging up the forest corridor.

A traveler need not be a prior believer in wilderness to see, after observing these abuses, that multiple use has been extended, or is planned to extend, or can extend on the personal whim of future Forest Service managers, *too far*. Where a bulldozer and chainsaw enter a valley, there is wilderness destroyed absolutely. But also, to the extent that sights and sounds of civilization intrude, wilderness is diminished in quality, and the places are becoming rapidly fewer in the North Cascades where one can get completely out of sight, out of sound, out of mind, of bulldozers and chainsaws, no matter how many days are devoted to respectful entry.

For those unfamiliar with multiple use in action, a visit to Mount Baker, especially from the Baker River side, is instructive. Here the primeval Baker Lake has been drowned by a fluctuating reservoir that has the same name but is not at all the same, no matter what the Forest Service multiple-users and the private power company kilowatt-producers say in their billboards and brochures. Here the road system is quite advanced, creeping far up the south slopes of Mount Baker, and also up the opposite side of the valley, and also to within several miles of Lake Anne, richly forested, and one can look in vain for any slope, any valley, that has been saved in its natural condition all the way from two-mile-high ice down to what not long ago was a virgin forest and wild river just 700 feet above the sea. Shuksan, often called "the most beautiful mountain in America," is almost completely ringed by logging roads. Here, on these two magnificent but unprotected peaks, one can learn that in essence multiple use means that no logging will be allowed above timberline.

To see what happens when a mountain-valley unit is sliced in half, saving only the ice and rock for recreation, and devoting all the trees to lumber production, one can visit the Mowich Lake entrance to Mount Rainier National Park, and on the way drive through miles and miles of privately owned stumps and fireweed, high onto buttresses of the very mountain. And to see what happens when not enough forests are saved to complement the ice and rock and flowers, one can visit the Paradise and White River entrances to Rainier Park, where the splendor and fame of the mountain is its own worst enemy, and there literally is not enough room within park boundaries to provide sufficient camping space, and thus it is necessary—unless every remaining tree is to be sacrificed—to build such facilities outside the park. And to see the Forest Service extending multiple use of public land onto the mountain, one can visit the Carbon River entrance, and observe logging underway right up to the park boundaries, and just as high as marketable trees will grow.

There is more to multiple use than logging. At the abandoned mining town of Holden, on Railroad Creek, one can see a valley bottom, and a river, poisoned by the residues of an ore-concentrating plant that operated for some fifteen years—and visualize a similar operation on Miners' Ridge, and perhaps elsewhere in the North Cascades if it becomes the whim of the corporation miners now prospecting the range on foot and in helicopters, subsidized by the depletion allowance, and thus by every American taxpayer.

At numerous places one can see the damage done by little mines, in some cases the work of honest speculators, but in several notorious examples never intended by their promoters to produce anything but the revenue from sale of stock certificates. Yet whether profitable or not, or honest or not, mining is sheltered by the benevolent umbrella of multiple use. It does not matter very much how individual Forest Service administrators feel about the miners, reputable or crooked, who stake their claims in the public land. The Service is bound to obey the Mining Act of 1872, as amended only very slightly since, and is almost completely at the mercy of the mining interests which uphold this ancient frontier law with extraordinary political strength, incredibly out of proportion to the number of people economically involved. This decrepit law must be changed, but it has not yet even been threatened by major reform, and so long as the miners have absolute dominion over the public domain—and under the terms of the 1964 Wilderness Act they retain this dominion even in dedicated Wilderness Areas until 1984 —no land under Forest Service management is safe; only in a properly dedicated national park can miners be made subservient to the larger national interest.

And for all the beauty of the meadows of the Napeequa, and of White Pass, they simply are not worth the hike during the summers when the Forest Service permits sheep to graze. In some areas where sheep are allowed, notably in the rolling highlands east of Lake Chelan, there is serious question whether particularly fragile meadows will long survive, or will be turned into alpine deserts.

Under the permissive doctrine of multiple use, *any* use, old or new, is worthy of acceptance into the canon, upon demand. Until the protests grew too great to be ignored, the Forest Service was developing plans to build a road down Bridge Creek to the Stehekin from the North Cross-State Highway, and went so far as to design the new Stehekin Campground with space for automobile trailers. The Service now says that it never *officially* planned a road into Stehekin, and argues against such a road, mildly. But it has not foresworn future logging in Bridge Creek, and once a logging road "to remove diseased trees and blow-downs," progresses some distance up the valley, within a few miles of the North Cross-State Highway, there would be no stopping it from completing the connection, and thus forever ruining the unique peacefulness of the Stehekin.

Even now motorized trail scooters are allowed along Bridge Creek, perhaps as the planned advance guard of logging trucks, though mechanized travel is barred on virtually all the rest of the Cascade Crest Trail, of which Bridge Creek is a part. It is instructive to observe the attitude of the Forest Service toward motorization, which many travelers of woods and hills consider to be a gross violation of the historical status quo. While excluding scooters from dedicated wilderness areas, the Service has not felt able, in all good multiple-use conscience, to bar them on principle. Signs forbidding machines have been posted on a few trails so rough scooter riders might fall off and get hurt, and on a few others where horse travelers have complained about the danger to life and limb, but in general the Service has placidly accepted people on wheels as the full equals of people on foot. In the six national forests west of the Great Plains, less than five percent of trails outside dedicated areas are closed to mechanical vehicles. Long-range planners of the Service, seeking a compromise between the racket of civilization and the sound of nature, have been caught in the act of toying with such absurd notions as building parallel trails, one for hikers, one for scooters, and building rugged scooter tracks that would specifically attract the hot-rods.

The noise on the roads and trails is paralleled potentially by noise in the sky. Even without highways, the quiet of the high hills would in time be destroyed by increasing, tolerated use of airplanes—which already fly regularly to the town of Stehekin and to various alpine lakes—and of helicopters, which are now too expensive for all but corporation miners supported by the depletion allowance, but with increasing traffic by fishermen and goat-hunters and the like might soon become a threat to the privacy of all walkers of unprotected wilderness.

There is only one way to halt the continuing nibbles and gulps of multiple use, and that is through the creation of a national park—and a national park now—not twenty years from now. The Forest Service plans for the North Cascades are a matter of public record, and they do not encompass full and proper protection of all the scenic heartland that deserves and demands preservation as a parkland with a wilderness core and with a periphery of wilderness thresholds appropriate to the core.

In the view of the Forest Service, the existing Glacier Peak Wilderness, established in 1960, in company with a new wilderness to be reclassified from the existing North Cascades Primitive Area, will amply serve the nation's needs for wilderness in the North Cascades, and the remainder of the region should be devoted to multiple use, with emphasis on recreation (including roads, resorts, ski tows, and tramways) but with logging allowed in out-of-the-way nooks, and also such mining as is legal, and also grazing in most places where it now exists.

It is obvious that the Forest Service, in the worthy attempt to become closely responsive to local needs, has become provincial, and forgetful of national needs. The Service steadily treats the North Cascades as a matter concerning Bellingham, Wenatchee, and perhaps secondarily Seattle. What have Portland, San Francisco, Chicago, New Orleans, New York, and Boston to do with the North Cascades?

The Forest Service has also proven itself unable to comprehend that the generous size of the North Cascades wilderness is no reason to diminish it, but rather all the more reason to preserve its full immensity. That this much primitive land has lingered so late in history is a matter of luck—and the lucky chance should not be tossed away, but should be exploited by setting aside a wilderness large enough to remain genuinely wild, to contain its own built-in protection.

The Glacier Peak Wilderness established by the Forest Service in 1960 is *not* large enough, and does not even sufficiently guard the mountain itself, as especially evidenced by the logging in the White Chuck.

And the entire region from Cascade Pass north to the North Cross-State Highway, including all the giant peaks and enormous valleys centered on Eldorado and Park Creek Pass, is currently given only the tenuous protection of a "recreation area" where the logging won't be quite so flagrant as in other multiple-use areas.

On these points the Forest Service is *wrong*.

The alternative is a North Cascades National Park, a park with a wilderness core much larger than the existing Glacier Peak Wilderness, a park with a North Cascades Parkway across its northern edge rather than a North Cross-State Logging Road, a park with the wilderness fringes and thresholds protected for their scenery, a park with Lake Chelan preserved as a supreme water-road approach to the Stehekin—a North Cascades National Park created not in the distant future, when mere scraps remain as reminders of what has been lost, but *now* while there is still something—still much, very much—to save.

In a bleak time, when a week of rain is a year,
The slag-heaps fume at the edge of the raw cities:
The gulls wheel over their singular garbage;
The great trees no longer shimmer;
Not even the soot dances.

ROBERT F. FRENKEL. *Logging and burning, Newhalem Creek, 1959, a continuing operation in what was proposed for a park*

And the spirit fails to move forward,
But shrinks into a half-life, less than itself,
Falls back, a slug, a loose worm
Ready for any crevice,
An eyeless starer.

RICHARD BROOKS: *White Chuck Valley and Glacier Peak, logged in 1942, photographed in 1957*

DAVID SIMONS: *Trapper Lake*

I would be a stream, winding between great striated rocks in late summer;
A leaf, I would love the leaves, delighting in the redolent disorder of this mortal life,
This ambush, this silence,
Where shadow can change into flame,
And the dark be forgotten.

Part II

A HALF-CENTURY AGO a historic confrontation took place between two men, Gifford Pinchot and John Muir, over the future of Hetch Hetchy Valley in the Sierra Nevada. Both were influential leaders in the growing conservation movement, and more often in agreement than conflict, united as they were in opposing the rapacious exploitation of public lands practiced by frontier and post-frontier entrepreneurs. However, on Hetch Hetchy they split irreconcilably, Pinchot favoring the flooding of the valley to provide San Francisco with a water supply, Muir protesting that a water supply could be obtained elsewhere, but not another Hetch Hetchy, which in its primeval state was a second Yosemite. Pinchot won that argument, and Muir lost, but few admirers of Pinchot are now proud of his victory, and Muir's defeat has since been put to good use by his followers, who time and again—and now in the North Cascades—have faced the same short-sightedness evidenced by Pinchot at Hetch Hetchy.

It is grossly oversimplifying the historical contributions of these two complex men to speak of them solely in terms of this one incident. But it was a classic battle, and in many ways parallel to the current conflict between their followers in the North Cascades, a conflict Linnie Marsh Wolfe has described as between "the strictly utilitarian, commercial group who followed Pinchot, and the aesthetic-utilitarian group who followed Muir...."

Pinchot, the first Chief of the Forest Service, expressed his position by saying, "The object of our forest policy is not to preserve the forests because they are beautiful... or because they are refuges for the wild creatures of the wilderness... but... for the making of prosperous homes ... Every other consideration comes as secondary." His ideals, as elaborated and extended by his successors, are those ultimately codified in the Multiple Use Act passed by Congress in 1960.

Muir, on the other hand, while agreeing that most public lands should be devoted to the bread-and-butter needs of man, maintained that some scenic climaxes are of such higher value that no matter what their market price they should be preserved for human needs above the level of bread and circuses. His ideals are those expressed in the National Park Act of 1916, drafted primarily by Frederick Law Olmsted, *fils*, and the Wilderness Act of 1964, drafted primarily by Howard Zahniser.

During the 1920's the "aesthetic-utilitarian group" had considerable influence within the Forest Service. Impelled by such men as Aldo Leopold, and probably spurred by a Coolidge Administration plan to expand national parks, the Gila Wilderness Area was dedicated and the "L Regulations" adopted, providing for primitive areas with minimal road construction and other human disturbance. However, the "strictly utilitarian, commercial" viewpoint was not thereby renounced or even damaged, since the lands so set aside had little if any economic values then feasible to exploit. Indeed, in some parts of the nation holders of private timberlands were insisting that public logs be kept off the market, and their political power represented a potential danger to the very existence of the Service. Furthermore, the National Park Act of 1916 had taken the parks away from the Forest Service, transferring them to the Park Service; additional losses were feared, and the "L Regulations" were extensively utilized in attempts to maintain jurisdiction over areas of particular scenic distinction.

The national park concept gained enormously in support during the 1920's, threatening the Forest Service at numerous points. To combat one of these threats, in 1931 the Service established the Glacier Peak Recreation Area of 233,600 acres, mainly above timberline—hoping by this small gesture to relieve the pressure for a park which had been building since 1906, when the Mazamas made the first proposal, and since 1916, when Stephen Mather, first Director of the National Park Service, visited the region, and 1917, when Mary Roberts Rinehart predicted a park within a year, and 1919, when the Yakima and Spokane Chambers of Commerce called for a park, and the entire decade of the 1920's when The Mountaineers repeatedly drew attention to the area, and since 1929, when Williard Van Name, in his famous book, *The Vanishing Forest Reserves*, reiterated the demand.

The next years, those of the New Deal, were difficult for the "strictly utilitarian, commercial" group in the Forest Service. In 1933 the "Copeland Report" (*A National Plan for American Forestry*, see Bibliography) exposed the mess private forestry was in, analyzed defects in public forestry practices, and made new proposals—including those of Robert Marshall—for wilderness areas and national parks and monuments. Out of this came a revolt within the influential Society of American Foresters that led President Roosevelt to appoint as Chief Forester Ferdinand A. Silcox, who sympathized to a considerable extent with the "aesthetic-utilitarian" philosophy.

Also in 1933, under the Roosevelt Administration and the vigorous leadership of Secretary of the Interior Harold L. Ickes, there at last took place the long-feared transfer of the national monuments to the Park Service. And in 1938 Olympic National Park was created, including not only the Mount Olympus National Monument established in 1915, but much surrounding land that the Forest Service attempted to retain by placing it, in 1936, within primitive areas. In 1940 Kings Canyon National Park was established on what had been national forest lands—again under Ickes' leadership—a park which to this day has retained virtually all its wilderness.

In 1937 Secretary Ickes, in planning for a number of other new national parks, authorized a preliminary study of the Cascades. From this study, directed by O. A. Tomlinson, Superintendent of Mount Rainier National Park, came a proposal for an Ice Peaks National Park extending along the range from Mounts St. Helens and Adams to the Canadian border, including all the volcanoes and substantial wilderness hinterlands.

Battle lines were complex in the late 30's. Though the frontier ethic continued to rule in commercial circles, public opinion and governmental strength now supported the "aesthetic-utilitarian" position with the full force of aroused national idealism. Unfortunately, the force was split. In the Park Service there were heirs of Muir proposing Olympic National Park and Ice Peaks National Park. Threatened by so many park proposals, the Forest Service could give free rein to the heirs of Muir within it. As a result,

the "U Regulations" were established, under which wilderness areas were set aside with stricter preservation criteria than those of primitive areas. Robert Marshall, who through the efforts of Roosevelt and Silcox had become Chief of the Division of Recreation Lands, was roving the national forests developing plans for an extensive wilderness system, including a 1938 proposal that 795,000 acres between the North Cascades Primitive Area and Stevens Pass—later known as the "Marshall-Silcox area"—be studied for possible wilderness classification.

There has been much speculation in the last quarter-century over how the Forest Service might have evolved had it not been for the tragic coincidence that in late 1939 both Ferdinand Silcox and Robert Marshall died. Some historians feel that had one or both lived even a few years longer the Service would now be quite unlike what it has become. However, the two men did die, prematurely, and a federal government preparing for war could spare no time for wilderness.

The Ice Peaks National Park was defeated by the combined opposition of the Forest Service and of commercial interests in the State of Washington before conservationists in the state and nation were barely aware of the proposal, much less mobilized in its support.

And perhaps the first indication that the heirs of Pinchot were regaining control of the Forest Service was that in 1940 it summed up the North Cascades episode by setting aside not 795,000 acres, but only 352,000 acres, and not as a Glacier Peak Wilderness Area but as a Glacier Peak Limited Area—a classification that has been described by a Service employee as meaning "We haven't yet figured out where to put the logging roads."

The 1940's, years of war and readjustment for the nation, were years of consolidation for the "strictly utilitarian, commercial" foresters of the Pinchot school. The growing demand for public timber strengthened their hand, and the defeat of the park threat obviated their need to go along, for strategic reasons, with proposals for wilderness emanating from "aesthetic-utilitarians." The wave of thought typified by Bob Marshall had been contained and could now be gradually, subtly suppressed. In 1940, with Silcox and Marshall gone, the Forest Service began to move into its present period of monolithic unanimity.

However, the Service continued to benefit from the work and ideas of Leopold and Marshall and Silcox. Many travelers of the North Cascades contrasted the wilderness they experienced there with conditions in certain overcrowded national parks where distraught, misguided officials had deviated from the ideals of the National Park Act and made too many concessions to recreation, at the expense of the natural scene. The Forest Service took full advantage of this distrust of national parks, and has continued to do so, pointing with justifiable pride to its pioneer work in setting aside primitive areas and wilderness areas—though failing to mention that for three decades it has not added substantially to its wilderness system, but rather during this period has steadily eroded the legacy of the Marshall era.

When public interest in the North Cascades reawakened in the early 1950's, many adherents of Muir who remembered Marshall felt the wilderness was safest with the Forest Service. During the next decade the Service moved steadily to disillusion them.

In 1951, with the demand for public logs growing as privately owned old-growth forests dwindled, it was at last possible for the Forest Service to develop management plans for its hitherto unexploitable back country. Thus, in that year, the Service announced that preliminary studies would soon begin on reclassification of the Glacier Peak Limited Area.

With no further action having been taken by 1955, and knowing that a "limited area" was no permanent protection at all, the Federation of Western Outdoor Clubs urged the Forest Service to begin these long-overdue studies, and specifically recommended that the "Marshall-Silcox area" be designated as a wilderness. In response to a reiteration of this request by The Mountaineers, in April 1955, the Service made public, in February 1957, its Glacier Peak Land Management Study.

Meanwhile logging was proceeding in valleys felt by conservationists to deserve inclusion in the proposed wilderness. Some among them recognized the public was not getting objective judgments and that a fresh viewpoint by "aesthetic-utilitarians" was needed to balance the "strictly utilitarian, commercial" orientation increasingly evidenced by the Forest Service. One of them, the late David Simons, in a November 1956 letter to Senator Kuchel of California, interceded for help in obtaining a study of the North Cascades by an inter-agency group. Senator Kuchel forwarded the letter, and in December the Chief Forester answered that no such study by any other agency was required, since the area was the sole responsibility of the Forest Service, which was discharging its responsibility.

Disturbed by the adamant refusal of the Forest Service to cease logging in scenic areas and to allow any outside agency to review its policies, in 1957 a group of Northwest residents founded the North Cascades Conservation Council to arouse public interest in the need for reform.

That reform was badly needed was made abundantly evident by the Glacier Peak Land Management Study completed by the Service in February 1957, a study that consisted mainly of resource maps giving no special attention to scenic qualities, and tentatively proposing a mere 434,000-acre "Marshall-Silcox wilderness, as contrasted to the 795,000-acre "Marshall-Silcox area." The study offered no clues as to how the data on the maps related to the conclusions concerning the proposed wilderness, but it was evident that the chosen boundaries excluded virtually all timber of any great commercial value.

After two more years of hearing both sides of the question, in February 1959 the Forest Service announced its reduced proposal of 422,925 acres—a star-fish wilderness confined to tentacle-like ridges of rock and snow emanating out from Glacier Peak, with intervening forested valleys devoted to commercial development—wilderness-on-the-rocks that excluded the valleys of the Suiattle, White Chuck, and White Rivers, and Phelps and Agnes Creeks, as well as the entire area from Cascade Pass to the Skagit River.

Taking a long look at the appallingly inadequate proposal, Congressman Thomas Pelly of Seattle concluded that the Service was incompetent to evaluate scenic values and wrote the Director of the National Park Service, in March 1959, asking for an independent evaluation of the area and asking nineteen specific questions, particularly requesting the Park Service to indicate which valleys or portions of valleys between Stevens Pass and the Skagit River should, in its opinion, be released for commercial use and which protected for the sake of scenery, and also which should be preserved in a wilderness condition and which developed for road-side recreation.

As required by statute, the Director of the Park Service requested permission from the Chief of the Forest Service to conduct such a study. When no answer was received by the Director, Congressman Pelly wrote directly to the Chief. In August 1959 the Chief replied, and again, as in 1956, denied the request. The Congressman then introduced into the 86th Congress, and also into the 87th, a bill to require a North Cascades study.

Congressman Pelly's misgivings were widely shared. At public hearings held that fall in Bellingham and Wenatchee, testimony went three to one against an emasculated Glacier Peak Wilderness Area, and the protest forced a retreat, however modest, from the "star-fish" proposal. In his order of September 6, 1960, setting aside a 458,505-acre Glacier Peak Wilderness Area, the Secretary of Agriculture rejected Forest Service recommendations by completely closing to logging the disputed corridors of the upper Suiattle, Agnes, and Phelps. Also in opposition to Service desires, he ordered that the country northward from Cascade Pass, though omitted from the wilderness, should be managed primarily for recreation and scenic preservation, with logging allowed only when compatible with these aims. There was a catch with respect to the Suiattle; its retention as wilderness was assured only so long as the Miner's Ridge-Plummer Mountain mining claims remained economically unattractive.

The following June a new Secretary of Agriculture intervened to restrict even further the freedom of Forest Service action. Responding to requests by Senators Jackson and Magnuson of Washington, and Senators Morse and Neuberger of Oregon, in June 1961 Secretary Orville Freeman imposed a general moratorium on logging in certain areas of the two states, including the area between Cascade Pass and Ruby Creek, until a policy was worked out for protection of the scenery, and instructed the Service to prepare a general plan for preserving the landscapes of all the high mountains throughout Oregon and Washington.

The Forest Service dutifully obeyed the letter, if not the spirit, of Secretary Freeman's directive, in March 1962, with a "High Mountain Policy" that provided for "Landscape Management Areas" around certain lakes, rock outcrops, and principal recreation access corridors, these to be managed to yield half to two-thirds of the normal log harvest, with scenery to appear unimpaired from major roads and trails. There was actually nothing new in the policy, which was little more than a broadening of the traditional policy of preserving roadside strips and a restatement of Regulation U-3, which defines multiple-use areas with emphasis on recreation. Scenery was still forced to prove its case against all other uses. In the specific places since designated as "Landscape Management Areas," all the trees will ultimately be logged, but less rapidly—that is, where the log yield has been reduced to half of normal for the sake of scenery, the Service will take twice as long to cut the trees—but cut them all it will.

Because the enunciation of the High Mountain Policy signaled the end of the 1961 moratorium, in June 1962 Congressman Pelly asked Secretary Freeman for a new moratorium on logging below 4,000 feet in twenty key valleys of the North Cascades. The Secretary's office replied in September that no logging was planned in ten of the areas for five years, but affirmed the Forest Service's insistence on resuming logging immediately in the other ten valleys.

This answer reflected an incomplete understanding of the urgency of the situation. After further explanation of the nature of the problem, in January 1963 Secretary of Agriculture Orville Freeman joined with Secretary of the Interior, Stewart Udall, in authorizing a joint inter-departmental study of the management and administration of federal lands in the North Cascades, as conservationists had been requesting since 1956.

Realizing that this joint evaluation might well lead to a revision of policies permitting wholesale logging, in February 1963 Congressman Pelly renewed his moratorium request. This time the Secretary of Agriculture responded by implying a partial moratorium, saying that no new timber sales would be scheduled during the remainder of the year in eight of the ten areas still subject to logging, and that he would review the matter at the beginning of the following year. However, the Forest Service had persuaded him that time was too short to find replacement sales for those already scheduled within the White Chuck critical area, and thus the logging on the White Chuck (Meadow Mountain) and Suiattle (Green Mountain) was allowed to proceed as planned.

Meanwhile, since 1963 the North Cascades Study Team, consisting of Chairman Edward C. Crafts, Director of the Bureau of Outdoor Recreation, Arthur Greeley, Jr. of the Forest Service, George Selke, consultant to George Hartzog, Director of the Park Service, and Owen Stratton of Wellesley College, has been developing a report orginally promised for January 1965 but now scheduled for release in the summer of 1965.

It was the general understanding among members of the public, and their representatives in Congress, that the spirit underlying the North Cascades study was that of the so-called "Treaty of the Potomac," an apparent pledge to President Kennedy by the federal agencies involved that they would not enter into controversies concerning the long-range status of the North Cascades, especially while the study was in progress.

However, in March 1965, with the Study Team's report momentarily expected, the Forest Service abruptly announced a 500,000-acre "Eldorado Peaks Recreation Area" extending from Cascade Pass to the Skagit River—closely approximating the northern segment of the proposed North Cascades National Park. And though only a small portion of the lands in three national forests is involved, administrative teams from five national forests in Washington State preciptiously began an intensive publicity campaign, sending out speakers with slide shows and pamphlets to carry the message to any group willing to listen.

When conservationists strenuously objected to the timing of the announcement, calling it a flagrant attempt to undercut the Study Team, Forest Service spokesmen denied any breach of faith, insisting it was a coincidence they chose this particular time to publicize long-range plans which had been in preparation for years. Under questioning they further denied that there was any such entity as an "Eldorado Peaks Recreation Area,"—and well they might, since the Service's own regulations require that a recreation area of this size can only be established by order of the Secretary of Agriculture after certain specified hearings and studies. Since the "Recreation Area" is not legally one, why call it that? The Service implies the term is used in a figurative sense to help the public understand the management plans. However, by making the announcement at this time, in these terms, with such emphasis, the Service makes it easy to infer that the clear intent is to obscure the North Cascades Study Team recommendations, whatever they might be, by raising a cloud of dust in advance.

Until 1960, many conservationists of the "aesthetic-utilitarian" school hoped to obtain protection of the North Cascades under Forest Service administration, and placed their hopes in a Glacier Peak Wilderness of sufficient dimensions to do the job properly. However, the total inadequacy of the area as established, and repeated refusals to consider wilderness classification for the Cascade Pass-Skagit River area, led these conservationists to join with others who all along had been proposing another solution, that of a national park. After intensive studies and discussions, in 1963 the North Cascades Conservation Council published its *Prospectus for a North Cascades National Park*, and the proposal outlined therein has been endorsed by the Sierra Club, The Mountaineers, the Mazamas, the Cascadians, the National Parks Association, the Wilderness Society, the Federation of Western Outdoor Clubs, and other groups and individuals.

The proposed park would, above all, be wilderness, and guaranteed as such by statute—extending over a much broader region the protection now given to the immediate vicinity of Glacier Peak. (See boundaries on the map enclosed in the back pocket of this book.) Most existing roads would be maintained, but no major new penetrations would be allowed, with the exception of the North Cross-State Highway (in any event too far advanced to be stopped) which would be a North Cascades Parkway. Any other new roads would be limited to the periphery. Similarly, existing trails would be maintained, and some new ones built, but most of the back country would remain completely natural. Campgrounds would be provided along existing roads, and visitors' information centers established at major entrances, but commercial development would be left to the gateway towns outside the park, except for private facilities in the town of Stehekin and other existing enclaves of civilization.

Fishing would continue in the park, as it does in all parks. Hunting would not. However, an integral part of the proposal is for an accompanying Chelan National Mountain Recreation Area, immediately adjoining the park on the east, where the scenery is in every respect of national park caliber, but hunting is a major and long-existing activity. The recreation area is proposed in order to allow hunting while giving, in every other respect, full national park protection.

Despite scare stories issued by the Washington State Game and Fish Department, which like the Forest Service habitually resists any effort to reduce its jurisdiction, the total proposal affects hunting to only a minor degree. The principal shooting areas have been placed in the recreation area, where shooting will continue. Within the proposed park itself, only some 800 deer are killed each year, roughly one per cent of the annual deer kill in the State of Washington, and a reduction easily replaced by a small increase that better management could bring in the allowable kill in areas adjacent to the park. The kill of goat and bear and other game is even less significant—to the hunter, that is, but not to those who value the experience of meeting animals in their wilderness condition.

Logging would cease both in the proposed park and recreation area, but the economic impact on the lumbering economy of the State of Washington would be slight, amounting to a reduction of only six per cent in the combined allowable cuts of the national forests involved, a minor figure compared to normal fluctuations in log production and frequent technical revisions in allowable cuts.

The loss of jobs supported by logging and other commercial activities would total approximately 314, compared to an estimated 2,095 new jobs created by 1980 through the enlarged tourism associated with the park. Other details of the park legislation would compensate local government for loss of tax and timber sales revenue during the early years of the park, and would ease the economic transition of the few individuals directly affected by its establishment.

In summary, the 1,038,665-acre North Cascades National Park and accompanying 269,521-acre Chelan National Mountain Recreation Area can be created without harming, but rather benefiting, the economy of the immediate locality and the state community.

However, the case for protecting this 1,300,000-acre region does not rest upon economics except to make clear that America can easily afford its preservation in a natural condition. Ultimately the case rests on whether the area is deserving, on its own merits, of national park status, and of that there can be no reasonable doubt.

This We Inherit

What time's my heart? I care.
I cherish what I have
Had of the temporal:
I am no longer young
But the winds and waters are;
What falls away will fall;
All things bring me to love.

ANSEL ADAMS: *On Bridge Creek*

ANSEL ADAMS: *Mount Booker, from Park Creek Pass*

I think of the rock singing, and light making its own silence,
At the edge of a ripening meadow, in early summer . . . .

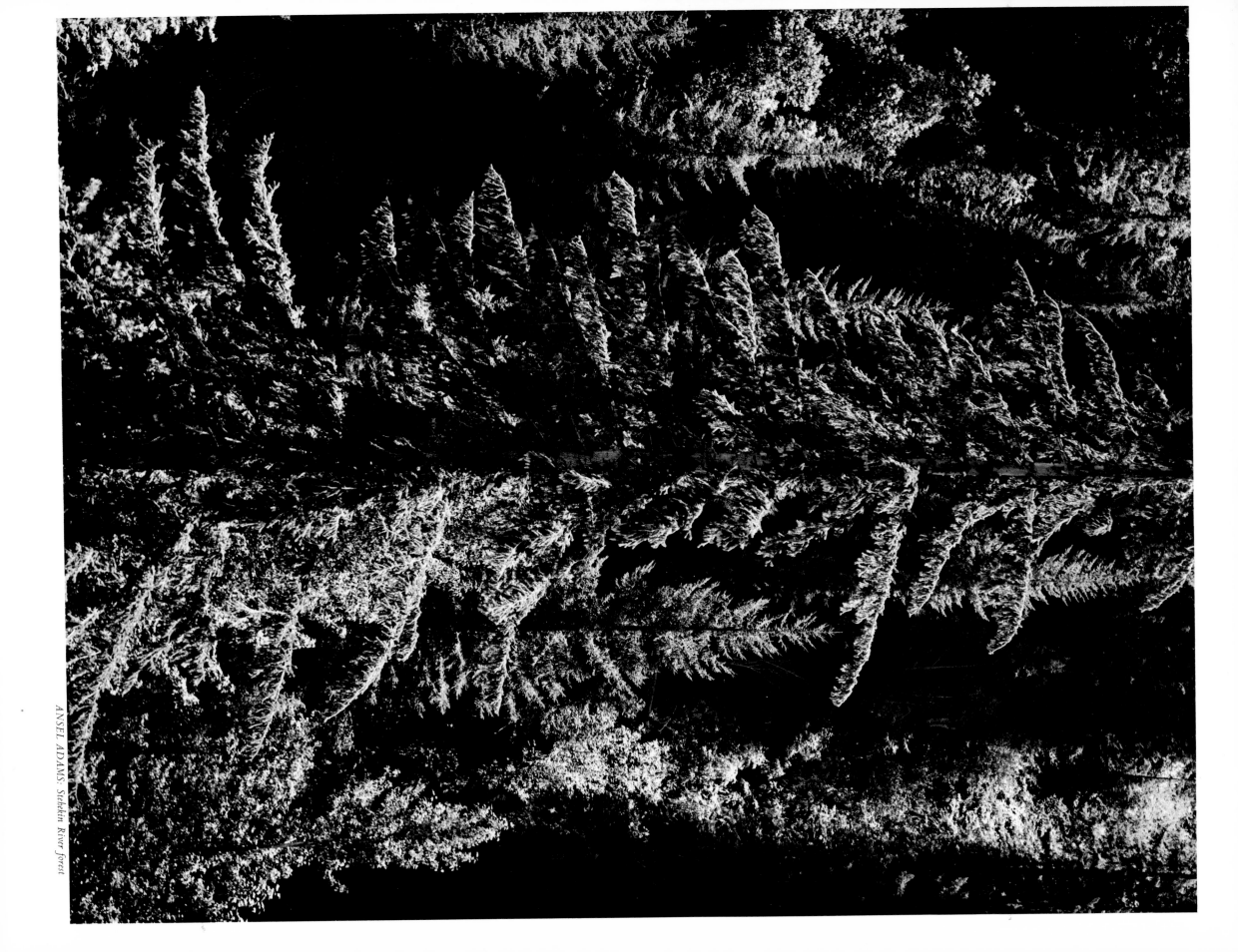

ANSEL ADAMS: *Stehekin River Forest*

The Visitant

1

A cloud moved close. The bulk of the wind shifted.
A tree swayed over water.
A voice said:
Stay. Stay by the slip-ooze. Stay.

Dearest tree, I said, may I rest here?
A ripple made a soft reply.
I waited, alert as a dog.
The leech clinging to a stone waited;
And the crab, the quiet breather.

2

Slow, slow as a fish she came,
Slow as a fish coming forward,
Swaying in a long wave;
Her skirts not touching a leaf,
Her white arms reaching towards me.

She came without sound,
Without brushing the wet stones,
In the soft dark of early evening,
She came,
The wind in her hair,
The moon beginning.

3

I woke in the first of morning.
Staring at a tree, I felt the pulse of a stone.
Where's she now, I kept saying.
Where's she now, the mountain's downy girl?

But the bright day had no answer.
A wind stirred in a web of appleworms;
The tree, the close willow, swayed.

ANSEL ADAMS: *Pool near Cascade Pass*

The bottom-stones shimmer back their irregular striations,
And the half-sunken branch bends away from the gazer's eye.
A scene for the self to abjure!—
And I lean, almost into the water,
My eye always beyond the surface reflection;
I lean, and love these manifold shapes . . .

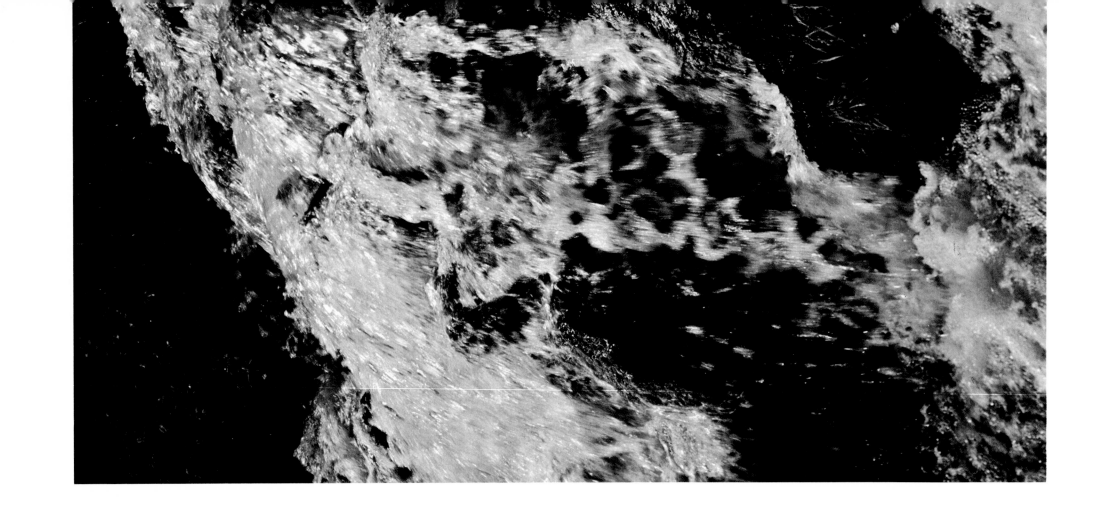

I learned not to fear infinity,
The far field, the windy cliffs of forever,
The dying of time in the white light of tomorrow,
The wheel turning away from itself,
The sprawl of the wave,
The on-coming water.

ANSEL ADAMS: *On Bridge Creek*

ANSEL ADAMS: *Talus*

Stupor of knowledge lacking inwardness—
What book, O learned man, will set me right?
Once I read nothing through a fearful night,
For every meaning had grown meaningless.
Morning, I saw the world with second sight,
As if all things had died, and rose again.
I touched the stones, and they had my own skin.

. . . I came upon the true ease of myself,
As if another man appeared out of the depths of my being,
And I stood outside myself,
Beyond becoming and perishing,
A something wholly other,
As if I swayed out on the wildest wave alive,
And yet was still.
And I rejoiced in being what I was . . .

REFERENCES

This list of references includes some of the major books, films, and articles from the publications shown. An extensive bibliography, including maps, technical publications, and articles in newspapers, is available through the Sierra Club.

Crowder, Dwight F. and Rowland Tabor. *Routes and Rocks: Hiker's Guide to the North Cascades Between Glacier Peak and Lake Chelan.* Seattle, The Mountaineers, 1965. Photographs, maps, drawings.

Douglas, William O. *My Wilderness: The Pacific West.* Garden City, New York, Doubleday and Co., 1960. Drawings.

Hazard, Joseph T. "Glacier Peak," *Snow Sentinels of the Pacific Northwest.* Seattle, Lowman and Hanford, 1932, pp. 113–31. Photographs.

McCloskey, J. Michael, ed. *Prospectus for a North Cascades National Park.* Seattle, North Cascades Conservation Council, 1963, Photographs, maps.

Manning, Harvey, ed. *Mountaineering: The Freedom of the Hills.* Seattle, The Mountaineers, 1960. Photographs, drawings. (Chapter 20, "Mountain Geology," deals in large part with the Northern Cascades).

Miller, Tom and Harvey Manning. *The North Cascades.* Seattle, The Mountaineers, 1964. Photographs, maps, drawings.

Peattie, Roderick, ed. *The Cascades.* New York, Vanguard Press, 1949.

Rinehart, Mary Roberts. *Tenting To-night: A Chronicle of Sport and Adventure in Glacier National Park and the Cascade Mountains.* Boston and New York, Houghton Mifflin Co., 1924. Photographs.

Rusk, Claude E. "Regal Glacier Peak, Ice-King of the Northern Cascades," *Tales of a Western Mountaineer, a Record of Mountain Experiences on the Pacific Coast.* Boston and New York, Houghton Mifflin Co., 1924.

Spring, Bob and Ira, with text by Byron Fish. *This is Washington.* Seattle. Superior Press, 1961. Photographs.

———, with text by Harvey Manning. *High Worlds of the Mountain Climber.* Seattle, Superior Press, 1959. Photographs.

Stegner, Wallace E. "An American Alps," *The American Heritage Book of Natural Wonders.* New York, American Heritage Publishing Co., 1963, pp. 272–73. Photographs.

Wills, Robert H. *High Trails, A Guide to the Cascade Crest Trail.* Seattle, University of Washington Press, 1962. Photographs, maps.

FILMS

Wilderness Alps of Stehekin, produced by David R. Brower, 16 mm., color, sound, 30 minutes. (Available: Sierra Club, San Francisco)

Wind in the Wilderness, produced by Bob Schulman, 16 mm, color, sound, 60 minutes. (Available from KING-TV, Seattle, Washington)

LIVING WILDERNESS

Brower, David R., "Crisis in the Northern Cascades," 68:35, Spring 1959.

Eighme, Lloyd E., "Through the Heart of the Northern Cascades," 26:9, Autumn 1948.

Heald, Weldon F., "The Chelan-Cascade Wilderness," 39:5, Winter 1951–52.

Marshall, Robert, "The Northern Cascades Wilderness," 1:10, September 1935.

Warth, John F., "Washington's Alpine Lakes Wilderness," 72:4+, Spring 1960.

Zahniser, Howard, "Wilderness in the Cascades," 58:ed. page, Fall-Winter 1956–57.

MAZAMA

Glisan, R. L., "Glacier Peak Outing of the Mazama Club," 4:1:6+, October 1912.

"Lake Chelan and Mt. Sahale," 2:138+, July 1903.

McFarland, G. L., "Back to the Chelan Country," 20:12:5+, 1938.

McNeil, Fred H., "In the Glacier Peak Region, 1926," 8:12:7+, 1926.

THE MOUNTAINEER

English, Edith Hardin, "Plant Life of the Area Surrounding Glacier Peak," 51:4:28, 1958.

Goldsworthy, Patrick D., "A Third National Park in Washington?", 54:5:4, 1961.

Hazard, Joseph T., "Let's Use the Cascade Crest Trail," 47:13:16, 1954.

McCloskey, J. Michael, "Major Policy Changes May Presage North Cascades National Park Legislation," 56:1:1, 1963.

McCloskey, J. Michael, "New Thoughts in Forest Recreation Theory," 57:7:12+, 1964 & 57:8:11+, 1964.

Meany, Edmund S., "Glacier Peak," 3:24+, 1910.

Misch, Peter, "Geology of the Northern Cascades of Washington," 45:13:4+, 1952.

Molenaar, Dee, "An Outline of the Geology of the Olympics and Cascades," 50:1:92+, 1956.

Nelson, L. A., "Records of Ascents of Glacier Peak," 3:25+, 1910.

Osseward, John, "Land Laws and Land Usage in Washington State," 54:4:69+, 1961.

SIERRA CLUB BULLETIN

Albright, Horace M., "More Park or All Forest: Highest Use vs Multiple Use," 45:4:3+, April-May 1960.

Brower, David R., "Crisis in the Northern Cascades, 'The Missing Million,'" 44:2:10+, February 1959.

———, "Golden Triangle of National Parks Proposed (Glacier Peak Hearing)," 45:1:7+, January 1960.

———, "Will We Discover the Northern Cascades in Time?" (Includes map and 19 plates by Philip Hyde and David Simons), 42:6:13, June 1957.

McConnell, Grant, "The Multiple-Use Concept in Forest Service Policy," 44:7:14+, October 1959.

Marshall, George, "Are These the New Criteria for Forest Wilderness?" 44:8:10+, November 1959.

Pelly, Thomas M., "Critically Important Letters Underline Cascades Problem," 45:3:4+, March 1960.

Ulrichs, Hermann F., "The Cascade Range in Northern Washington," 22:1:69, February 1937.

Zalesky, Philip H., and Founta Butler, "Economic Potential of Wilderness in the Northern Cascades," 44:7:29+, October 1959.

THE WILD CASCADES

Goldsworthy, Patrick D., "Washington's Golden Triangle of National Parks," 1, January 1960.

Hessey, Charles, "North Cascades Primitive Area," October 1958.

Zalesky, Philip H., "Statement by the North Cascades Conservation Council on the U.S. Forest Service Glacier Peak Wilderness Area Proposal," 1, March 1959.

GENERAL PUBLICATIONS

Goldsworthy, Patrick D., *Water Resources Management for the Needs of an Expanding Society,* "The Quality of the North Cascades," 61+, University of Washington, 1964.

Graves, C. Edward, "The Glacier Peak Wilderness," *National Parks Magazine,* 30:125:70, June 1956.

Heald, Weldon F., "The Undiscovered Cascades," *National Parks Magazine,* 33:145:8, October 1959.

Henderson, Kenneth A., "Sunshine and Storm in the Cascades," *Appalachia,* 8:39+, June 1942.

Irwin, Robert A., "Call to the Wilderness," 188+, *The World Book Encyclopedia, Yearbook—1956.* (North Cascades)

Kerouac, Jack, "Alone on a Mountaintop," *Holiday,* 24:68+, October 1958.

"Official Report of Proceedings Before the United States Department of Agriculture, Forest Service—In the matter of: The Proposed Establishment of Glacier Peak Wilderness Area." Bellingham, Washington, October 13, 1959 and Wenatchee, Washington, October 16, 1959.

"Our Wilderness Alps," *Sunset* 134:6, June 1965.

Park, Edwards, "Washington Wilderness, the North Cascades," *National Geographic,* 119:3:334+, March 1961.

Reich, Charles A., *Bureaucracy and the Forests,* The Fund for the Republic, 1962.

Rinehart, Mary Roberts, "A Pack Train in the Cascades," *Cosmopolitan,* August-September-October 1917.

Simons, David, *Brief: The Need for Scenic Resource Conservation in the Northern Cascades of Washington,* Sierra Club, 1958.